2003–2004 Annual Supplement to

THE PIANO BOOK

BUYING & OWNING A NEW OR USED PIANO

LARRY FINE

BROOKSIDE PRESS • BOSTON, MASSACHUSETTS

Brookside Press
P.O. Box 178, Jamaica Plain, Massachusetts 02130
(617) 522-7182
(800) 888-4741 (orders: Independent Publishers Group)

info@pianobook.com
www.pianobook.com

Printed in the United States of America

Distributed to the book trade by Independent Publishers Group,
814 North Franklin St., Chicago, IL 60610
(800) 888-4741 or (312) 337-0747

ISBN 1-929145-13-6 (print edition)
ISBN 1-929145-14-4 (electronic edition)

NOTICE

Reasonable efforts have been made to secure accurate information for this publication. Due in part to the fact that manufacturers and distributors will not always willingly make this information available, however, some indirect sources have been relied upon.

Neither the author nor publisher make any guarantees with respect to the accuracy of the information contained herein and will not be liable for damages—incidental, consequential, or otherwise—resulting from the use of the information.

INTRODUCTION

Given the long time span between new editions of *The Piano Book*, it's impractical to provide in the book itself the detailed model and price data that piano shoppers increasingly seek. Similarly, updated information about manufacturers and products is needed in a timely manner. This *Annual Supplement to The Piano Book*, published each summer, is designed to fill that information gap. I hope this modest companion volume will effectively extend the "shelf life" of *The Piano Book* as a valuable reference work, and serve as an additional information resource for piano buyers and piano lovers.

Larry Fine

June, 2003

CONTENTS

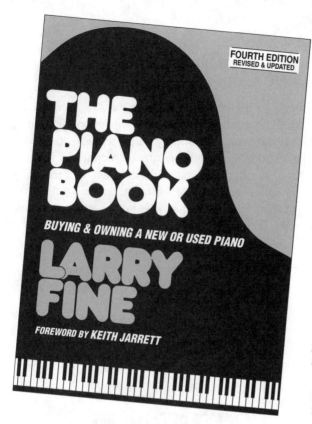

244 pages
8-1/2 x 11
100 line drawings

Paperback $19.95
Shipping/handling $5.00

- *Candid brand-by-brand reviews of new pianos*

- *Sales gimmicks to watch out for—and the real differences in piano quality and features*

- *How to negotiate the best deal*

- *Tips on finding, inspecting, appraising, and buying a used piano*

- *Special section on buying an older Steinway*

- *Piano moving, storage, tuning, servicing*

MANUFACTURER and PRODUCT UPDATE

This section describes changes to companies, products, and brand names since the fourth edition of *The Piano Book* went to press in the fall of 2000. This section is cumulative; that is, information contained in last year's *Supplement*, to the extent it is still accurate, is repeated here and changes that have occurred during the past year have been added. If a company or brand name is not listed here, it means that there is nothing new of substance to report.

It is not intended, of course, that the information in this update section take the place of the reviews in *The Piano Book*. With some exceptions, the update is limited to changes of a factual nature only, whereas the main book contains, in addition, critical reviews, ratings, and recommendations. Readers should understand that, in most cases, changes in the quality of any particular brand of piano occur very slowly, over a period of many years, if at all. Only where there has been an abrupt change in company ownership, or a period of rapid technological or economic change in the country of origin, is there likely to be a change in quality worth worrying about. For that reason, the reviews in *The Piano Book* can still be considered reliable unless otherwise noted here.

Trends

Pianos made in China continue to improve and make inroads into the North American market. By some estimates, more than one-quarter of all pianos sold in the U.S. in 2002 were made in China. As recently as 2001, most pianos from China, though technically acceptable, were not musically desirable. Last year the musical qualities took a big leap forward. Though nearly all makes have improved, special mention in this regard goes to the vertical pianos from the Yantai Longfeng factory, sold here under the Carl Ebel, Perzina, and Gerh. Steinberg labels, and the grands from Dongbei, sold under the names Nordiska, Everett, and Story & Clark, among others. Pearl River and Ritmüller pianos are also among the better ones. The jury is still out as to whether these pianos will hold up over the long term and in demanding climates and situations. Anecdotal reports, though encouraging, still suggest poorer quality control than with pianos from other countries. Prices are so low, however, that for many entry-level buyers these pianos are an excellent value despite some uncertainty about their longevity. At least as short-term investments, and in milder climates and less demanding situations, they are probably okay.

Although there has been an explosion of different brand names under which Chinese-made pianos are being marketed, there are only about eight Chinese manufacturers that make pianos for export to the U.S. Piano shoppers should keep in mind that, cosmetics aside, if two brands of piano originate in the same factory, they are probably very similar, if not identical.

On the other end of the price spectrum, European piano makers seem to be in a race to redesign their pianos for better sound projection and sustain, à la Steinway. The European piano market is dead, the U.S. market for high-end pianos is—relatively speaking—thriving, and for a number of companies, Steinway is the principal competitor. Considering how tradition-bound these companies are, this degree of activity is unusual. Some of the redesigns—new models from Seiler and Schimmel come to mind—have been terrific musical successes. My only worry is that the palette of available piano tonal qualities is becoming smaller and more homogeneous as the old-world sounds pass away.

ALTENBURG

Correction to web site address: www.altenburgpiano.com

The F.E. Altenburg line of pianos made by Niendorf is being discontinued.

ASTIN-WEIGHT

Change to web site address: www.astin-weight.com

New e-mail address: gr8pianos@networld.com

BALDWIN
including Chickering, Wurlitzer, Ellington, ConcertMaster

New address, phone, and ownership:

Baldwin Piano Company
309 Plus Park Blvd.
Nashville, Tennessee 37217

615-871-4500

Owned by: Gibson Piano Ventures, a wholly owned subsidiary of Gibson Guitar Corp.

Shortly after the fourth edition of *The Piano Book* was published in early 2001, the Baldwin board of directors hired a new management team to try to stave off impending bankruptcy caused by a series of costly mistakes and prior poor management. Avoiding bankruptcy turned out not to be possible, and the company filed for protection under Chapter 11 of the U.S. bankruptcy laws in May of 2001. On October 16, 2001, Baldwin's major creditor, General Electric Capital, purchased the company's assets at a court-ordered liquidation sale and then sold them to the Gibson Guitar Corporation on November 9, 2001.

Gibson owners Henry Juszkiewicz and Dave Berryman purchased Gibson in 1986 when it was in complete disarray and turned it into an extremely profitable and well-respected company. They feel that there are many parallels between Gibson's situation at that time and Baldwin's present situation, and expect to be able to turn Baldwin around as well.

Baldwin's new owners say they plan to make large capital investments to improve product quality. In addition they are reorganizing the Baldwin factories in Arkansas to once again produce grands in Conway and verticals in Trumann. This will result in the rehiring of many skilled workers who had been laid off when prior management consolidated most Baldwin manufacturing in the Trumann plant. The Juarez, Mexico action-making facility will also be reopened. A woodworking plant in Greenwood, Mississippi closed in mid-2000 will have its functions transferred to a new woodworking plant in Trumann for increased efficiency. A great cost savings will be realized by the transfer of all Baldwin sales, marketing, and administrative functions to Gibson headquarters in Nashville. Baldwin's line of digital pianos will be discontinued for the time being.

Prior to the management reorganization and subsequent bankruptcy, Baldwin had announced a number of changes to its product line, some of which were reported in *The Piano Book*. These changes were never fully realized due to the bankruptcy. The new owners plan to complete implementation of some of these changes (see comments below), and other changes are to be expected as Baldwin's reorganization evolves.

The Eurostyle consoles and studios (E100, E101, E102, E250, E260) have been discontinued.

In the grands, the new model 225E is the model M (5' 2") in French Provincial styling. The 7' model SF-10 has been renamed SF-10E in honor of its adoption of the enhanced features of the upgraded Artist series grands (see *The Piano Book* for details).

The Chickering grands reported on in *The Piano Book* have been withdrawn. They were to be replaced by three new models—5' 4", 5' 9", and 6' 2"—made by Samick in Korea, with some cosmetic features taken from old Chickering designs. Due to Baldwin's bankruptcy, however, Baldwin never took possession of these pianos, so they are being sold and warranted by Samick under license from Baldwin while supplies last. In my estimation, the quality should be much better than the Chickerings being withdrawn, probably comparable to other Samick-made instruments.

Baldwin has developed, and is now including, its new "Stealth"™ action in all vertical pianos. The "Full Blow" action, in use since 1939, has been updated with a Schwander-style hammer-butt return spring and other changes for improved quietness, responsiveness, durability, and ease of servicing. You can recognize the Stealth™ action by its visually striking deep blue color. In addition, pianos with the new action have model numbers ending in "E".

In the grand department, Baldwin has introduced a Custom Grand Finishes program, allowing customers to design their own grand piano. Four levels of customization are available: 1) wood-finish accents on regular grands; 2) colors (Jubilee Red, Golden Honey, Evergreen, Beale Street Blue, Madeira); 3) exotic wood veneers; and 4) anything you want.

Baldwin has reintroduced the Ellington brand name on a line of pianos made in China. The original Ellingtons were produced by Baldwin from 1893 to 1930 as its lower-priced alternative to the Baldwin line. Current Ellington verticals are made by the Beijing Piano Co. (see "Beijing"), grands by Sejung (see "Sejung"). The verticals are available in both continental and American furniture styles, have a laminated spruce soundboard, and come with a ten-year parts and labor warranty. The industry's only spinet piano is part of this line (formerly part of the Wurlitzer line). Also noteworthy is the Ellington model 100 MelodyMaker, a 73-note, compact vertical piano. The company says that except for the number of notes, this is a true acoustic piano with all the features of a full-size piano. The grands, 4' 7" and 5' 1", have a solid spruce soundboard and a ten-year parts and labor warranty.

As for Baldwin's Wurlitzer line of pianos, the verticals have been discontinued (essentially replaced by the Ellington line). The grands are still made in Korea by Samick, but most have been renumbered with model numbers beginning with WP. They will be sold while supplies last, and Baldwin will announce later this year its future plans for the brand name.

When Gibson acquired Baldwin, it acquired only its assets, not its liabilities. Therefore, the company is not required to honor warranty claims for pianos purchased prior to the acquisition date. Pianos purchased by the consumer on or after November 9, 2001 are eligible for warranty coverage, even if the dealer purchased the piano before that date. Warranty coverage for pianos purchased by the consumer before November 9, 2001 will only be considered on a case-by-case basis.

In mid-April 2002, Baldwin cancelled agreements with most of its dealers, retaining only the most active ones. The company says it intends to rebuild its dealer network, inviting new dealers to demonstrate their commitment, in part by making large purchases from the company. Baldwin says, however, that it *will* honor the warranty on pianos purchased from "cancelled" dealers, even though, technically, they are no longer "authorized" dealers.

Gibson appears to have a reasonable chance to turn Baldwin around. The company also has a good track record with regard to continued ownership of other acquired companies and the honoring of their warranties. Nevertheless, such undertakings are obviously not without risk. Therefore, I would advise purchasers of Baldwin products to obtain a written warranty from the dealer covering parts and labor for at least ten years in addition to whatever manufacturer's warranty may come with the product.

BECHSTEIN, C.

New North American distributor:

SMC (formerly Samick Music Corp.)
18521 Railroad Street
City of Industry, California 91748

626-964-4700
800-592-9393
www.bechstein.de

Korean piano maker Samick has purchased a majority interest in C. Bechstein by acquiring the shares held by Karl Schulze, Bechstein's largest shareholder. Schulze also purchased a fifteen percent interest in Samick. Samick will help Bechstein increase production and diversify its product line, and Bechstein will help Samick market its pianos in Europe. Bechstein will remain as a separately managed German corporation.

Bechstein has introduced a new series of very beautiful designer verticals called "ProBechstein" in 45½", 46½", and 49" sizes. In the Pricing Guide section, they are the models called "Balance," "Avance," and "Ars Nova."

The 9' 2" model D-280 concert grand has been redesigned, with a capo bar and duplex scale in the treble for better tonal projection. Also, unlike most other Bechsteins, which utilize an open pinblock design, this concert grand plate covers the pinblock area. These features have also been added to the 6' 2" model M/P-192 grand and will soon be added to the B-210 (6' 11") and the C-232 (7' 6") models.

SMC, Samick's North American distribution arm, will market and distribute Bechstein pianos in the U.S. and Canada. Plans call for reintroducing the "Bechstein" (as opposed to "C. Bechstein") brand name. Under the name "C. Bechstein," SMC will distribute the three "ProBechstein" verticals, the 51-1/2" Concert vertical, and the newly-designed grand models mentioned above. Under the name "Bechstein," SMC will distribute the older, unenhanced versions of these grands, namely models 160 (5' 3"), 180 (5' 11"), 190 (6' 3"), and 208 (6' 10"). The various models will be phased in gradually during 2003 and 2004.

The W. Hoffmann line of pianos has been discontinued in the U.S. and Canada. A version of this piano from the same factory (Bohemia) will continue to be sold here under the "Bohemia" name by the Bohemia Piano Co. (see "Bohemia").

BECKER, J.

All J. Becker verticals now feature agraffes throughout the scale.

BEHNING

See "Weber"

BEIJING XINGHAI

Beijing Piano Factory, part of the Beijing Xinghai Musical Instruments Co., has been producing pianos since 1949 and manufactures more than fifty thousand vertical and grand pianos annually. They are available throughout the world under the Otto Meister and Xinghai labels, as well as under various other labels as joint ventures with other manufacturers and distributors, including Heintzmann (in Canada), Ellington (Baldwin), Story & Clark, and Wyman. Kawai also has a joint venture with Beijing, though the pianos are distributed only in Canada and Europe, not the U.S. (at one time they bore the name "Linden").

The assets of Canadian piano manufacturer Heintzman were purchased by a Chinese company and moved from Canada to Beijing, where pianos are now produced under the Heintzman name in joint venture with the Beijing Piano Factory by a firm known as Beijing Heintzman. Prices were not available at press time. Although information about these pianos is scarce, my sources tell me that the quality is a little higher than that of some of the other Beijing-made pianos.

BERGMANN

See "Young Chang"

BLONDEL, G.

Distribution of Blondel pianos in the U.S. has been discontinued.

BLÜTHNER

In honor of the company's 150th anniversary, Blüthner has introduced a Jubilee model which has a commemorative cast-iron plate in the style of the special-edition pianos of a century ago. Any grand piano model can be special-ordered with this commemorative plate.

In what is perhaps a world's "first," Blüthner has designed and built a piano for left-handed pianists. This is a completely "backwards" piano, with the treble keys, hammers, and strings on the left and the bass on the right. When it was introduced, a pianist gave a concert on it after only a couple of hours of practice! It is currently available in the 6' 10" and 9' 2" sizes by special order (price not available).

BOHEMIA (new listing)

German American Trading, Inc.
P.O. Box 17789
Tampa, Florida 33682

813-961-8405
germanamer@aol.com

Pianos made by: Bohemia Piano Co., Hradec Kralove, Czech Republic.

The factory that makes Bohemia pianos began production in 1871, after World War II becoming part of the Czech state-owned enterprise that included the better-known Petrof. Privatized in 1993, Bohemia now makes

2,000 verticals and 300 grands per year. Originally it exported to the U.S. under the name Rieger-Kloss (now discontinued), first making only verticals, then adding grands made with Young Chang rims, and now making the entire instrument in its own factory. The name Bohemia is derived from the original term used by the ancient Romans for the part of Europe that is now the Czech Republic.

Specifications for the instruments include solid spruce soundboards, sand-cast plates, either Czech Detoa actions or Renner parts on Bohemia action frames (the latter denoted by "BR" in model numbers), either Renner or Abel hammers, and either Detoa or Kluge keyboards. All pianos come with a leather upholstered adjustable artist bench.

The Bohemia grands I played at a trade show sounded and felt very good, with a nice, bright, singing treble tone.

Warranty: Ten years, parts and labor.

BÖSENDORFER

New U.S. distributor address, phone, and e-mail:

Bösendorfer USA
577B Hackman Road
Lititz, Pennsylvania 17543

888-936-2516
bosendorferusa@aol.com

In January 2002, Bösendorfer was purchased from Kimball International by the BAWAG - P.S.K. Group, Austria's third largest banking group. Bösendorfer has a special place in Austrian history and culture, and although the company has thrived under Kimball's ownership, for some time there has been a desire on all sides to return Bösendorfer to Austrian hands. The new owner says it intends to maintain the same high standards of material and workmanship for which the company is renowned. It will also continue the new marketing course of the last few years, including the redesign of existing models, a new "Artisan" series of art case pianos, and the Conservatory series of cosmetically reduced, less expensive versions of its models.

In 2001, Bösendorfer introduced a new 9' 2" model 280 concert grand, and in 2002, a 6' 1" model 185 grand. These and other new and redesigned models share a new design philosophy in which the treble soundboard area is increased for better tonal projection by reducing excess cabinet distance between player and strings, and the bass soundboard area is increased for better bass response by joining the wide tail to the spine at a sharper corner.

The new concert grand is in addition to the two other concert grands (9' and 9' 6") the company already produces. Unlike the others, however, which have 92 and 97 keys, respectively, this new model has only 88 keys. Its scale design also features a front duplex and new action geometry. The company says the new model is intended for concert pianists who would otherwise be distracted or intimidated by the presence of additional keys in the bass. To my ears, the new piano has better sustain in the treble than I usually find in Bösendorfer pianos, but otherwise has a characteristic Bösendorfer sound and feel. The 9' model 275 is now available only by special order.

Bösendorfer showed several new models in 2003: a Porsche-designed modern piano suggestive of an automobile, a Victorian-styled piano called "Vienna," and two 175th anniversary models limited to a production run of 175 instruments each. The anniversary models, 52" model 130 and 5' 8" model 175, have such cosmetic enhancements as a burl walnut fallboard, gold trim, and a numbered medallion. Aside from the cosmetic enhancements, model 175 is the equivalent of a model 170 in the Conservatory series (not normally offered in this size), except with a high polish finish instead of satin.

The SE Reproducer system, out of production for a number of years, is back with updated electronics and solenoids. Bösendorfer says that the library for it will have top performers and that the system will play other disc formats as well.

BOSTON

The 49" vertical model UP-125 has been replaced with a completely redesigned 50" model UP-126. In the redesign, the wooden back has been made much heftier and the plate much more rigid to better resist torsional and bending stresses. Similar changes have also been made to the 52" model UP-132E (now 132E II), and the 46" model UP-118E (now 118E II). In the two larger models, the bass scale has been reworked with reduced string tension for smoother bass tone, and the soundboard taper and rib placement have been refined for better treble tone. Lastly, the music desk for the European-style case design has been improved so that it holds music more securely. Boston says it has plans to redesign the grands over time using the same structural analysis software employed in the design of its Essex line of pianos.

BREITMANN (new listing)

German Piano Imports LLC
5660 W. Grand River Ave.
Lansing, Michigan 48906

517-886-6000
800-954-3200
info@bluthnerpiano.com
www.bluthnerpiano.com

Pianos made by: Artfield Piano Ltd., Qing Pu, China

Breitmann is a brand associated with Blüthner and made in China. Features include Delignit pinblocks, German strings, Japanese hammers, and Renner parts in the grands.

THE BRITISH PIANO MANUFACTURING COMPANY LTD. (new listing)

This was, for a time, the new name for the company formerly known as Whelpdale, Maxwell & Codd. This company produced Welmar, Knight, Broadwood, Bentley, and Woodchester pianos. It purchased Woodchester in 2001 and moved the manufacturing facilities for all its brands to the Woodchester factory, formerly the Bentley factory (see *The Piano Book* for history).

In April, 2003, this company ceased operations. Its assets were purchased by a piano distributor in the United Kingdom, who said he has no immediate plans to reissue the brand names.

Clarification: In *The Piano Book* entry for Whelpdale Maxwell & Codd, I wrote that John Broadwood & Sons was established in 1728. It has been brought to my attention that this is not possible because Broadwood was not born until 1732. The 1728 (or 1729) date is widely used, however, and it probably represents the date of establishment of the shop of Burkat Shudi, with whom Broadwood apprenticed (1761), and of whose business Broadwood later became partner (1770) and, eventually, sole proprietor (1782).

CHASE, A. B. (new listing)

Musical Properties, Inc.
949 French Drive
Mundelein, Illinois 60060

773-342-4212

Pianos made by: Dongbei Piano Co., Dongbei, China

A. B. Chase is an old American piano name, formerly owned by Aeolian Pianos but to the best of my knowledge not used since that company's bankruptcy in 1985. Since 2001, the brand has been used by Musical Properties, Inc. on pianos from the Dongbei piano factory in China.

CHICKERING

See "Baldwin"

CABLE, HOBART M.

See "Sejung"

DISKLAVIER

See "Yamaha"

EBEL, CARL

See "Perzina, Gebr."

EISENBERG

See "Steinberg, Wilh."

ELLINGTON

See "Baldwin"

ESSEX

Steinway, through its Boston Piano Co. subsidiary, introduced several "Essex" models in early 2001 and 2002. These are manufactured in Korea by Young Chang. They include 5' 3" and 6' grands and 42", 44", and 48" verticals. The 42" and 44" vertical models are of identical scale design, but the smaller one is in a continental-style cabinet. Some of the vertical cabinets look backward to styles of past decades of the twentieth century.

15

The grands are available in both traditional and Art Deco styles, the difference being in the styling of the music desk.

Steinway says that it designed these pianos using state-of-the-art structural analysis software similar to that used in the auto and aircraft industries, allowing it to test the effects of a large number of variables in a short amount of time without having to build innumerable prototypes. Like Boston pianos, the Essex line was designed with a lower tension duplex scale and a larger, tapered solid spruce soundboard, for potentially better sustain. The grands utilize rosette-shaped flanges for better action stability.

ESTONIA

The name of the company has been changed to reflect its ownership by the Laul family.

New U.S. distributor contact information:

Laul Estonia Piano Factory
7 Fillmore Drive
Stony Point, New York 10980

845-947-7763
epfactory@aol.com
www.estoniapiano.com

The company reports that it has made a number of changes and improvements during the past two years, among which are: upgrading bass string making machinery; improving the method of drilling pinblocks; improving plate finishes; thicker inner rims on the 5' 6" grands; Renner Blue hammers on all models; establishing a quality control department headed by the elder Mr. Laul (both he and his wife are professional musicians); higher-grade and better-prepared veneers; and establishing a U.S. service center for warranty repairs. All pianos are now accompanied by a quality control certificate signed by a member of the Laul family.

Concerning the criticisms in *The Piano Book*, technicians report that Estonia pianos are now arriving at the dealer better prepared, and seem not to have problems anymore with uneven tuning pin tightness.

EVERETT

All Everett models are now made by the Dongbei Piano Co. in Dongbei, China.

FALCONE

See "Sejung"

FAZIOLI

Corrections to review: Three lids are optional on the 10' 2" grand. The 5' 2" and 6' models utilize a Delignit pinblock as mentioned, but the larger models have Bolduc (Canadian) pinblocks. The Fazioli warranty has been increased to ten years.

Additional web site address: www.fazioli.com

FEURICH

New U.S. representative:

Unique Pianos, Inc.
223 E. New Haven Avenue
Melbourne, Florida 32901

888-725-6633
321-725-5690
www.feurich.com

Pianos made by: Feurich Klavier-u.Flügelfabrikation GmbH, Gunzenhausen, Germany

This venerable German manufacturer is once again making pianos in its own factory. The models being offered at this time are 5' 8" (F172) and 7' 3" (F222) grands.

FÖRSTER, AUGUST

New web site address: www.august-foerster.de

GROTRIAN

Grotrian has introduced the Duo Grand Piano, two grand pianos placed side by side with keyboards at opposite ends, as in a duo piano concert, with removable rim parts, connected soundboards, and a common lid (price not available).

HALLET, DAVIS & CO.

Many of the Chinese-made Hallet & Davis pianos are now being made by the Dongbei Piano Co.

HAYDEN (new listing)

American Piano Distributors, Inc.
P.O. Box 21472
Roanoke, Virginia 24018

540-776-7900
888-MUSIC-12
Haydenmusic@aol.com
www.HaydenPiano.us

Pianos made by: Dongbei Piano Co., Dongbei, China

While Hayden pianos are currently manufactured by the Dongbei Piano Co., the distributor says it eventually plans to offer models from a number of different factories and countries.

HEINTZMAN

See "Beijing Xinghai"

HOFFMANN, W.

Bechstein has discontinued distribution of W. Hoffmann pianos in North America. Most of these instruments were manufactured by the Bohemia Piano Co. in the Czech Republic. Similar instruments are now being marketed in the U.S. under the Bohemia name by the manufacturer. See "Bohemia".

IBACH

New U.S. distributor information:

Resource West, Inc.
2295 E. Sahara Avenue
Las Vegas, Nevada 89104

702-457-7919
800-777-6874
info@ibachpiano.com
www.ibachpiano.com

The real German Ibach pianos are once again being distributed in the United States. Resource West says it will be distributing these fine pianos through interior design professionals and some smaller piano dealers. No investment is needed by the dealer. In lieu of stocking the pianos and receiving a regular retail markup, the dealer instead refers interested customers to the Resource West/Ibach showroom in Las Vegas and receives a substantial commission when a sale is made. Resource West prepares the pianos and delivers them to the customers. The price list in this *Supplement* is the suggested retail price at the Las Vegas showroom.

The Ibach-Daewoo joint venture mentioned in *The Piano Book* was discontinued and the Korean manufacturing operation was sold by Daewoo to an investment group that continued to manufacture pianos in Korea on a limited basis. These pianos were distributed for a time in the U.S. under the name Bachendorff (an arrangement now discontinued) and in Canada under the name Royale. At press time, a distributor operating under the name Persis International, Inc. says it will be having this Korean company make pianos under the Sohmer name (see "Sohmer").

IRMLER

The Chinese-made Irmlers have been discontinued. The European Irmlers are made in Poland with the technological assistance of Blüthner.

KAWAI

Additional web site address: www.shigerukawai.com

Kawai has opened a factory in Indonesia, where it will be making some piano models sold in the U.S., as well as cabinets and back assemblies for some models to be assembled in the U.S. Kawai also produces several vertical models in joint venture with the Beijing Xinghai Piano Co. in China. These pianos are sold in Canada and Europe, but not in the U.S. At one time these pianos bore the name "Linden", but use of that name has been discontinued.

True to its reputation, Kawai has made even more changes to its product line. The model 505 and 605 furniture-style consoles have been discontinued and replaced with several 44½" and 45" models utilizing the same scale design as the 605. Model 506 is this piano in a simple, studio-style cabinet, made in Indonesia. Although called a "studio" because of the cabinet style, it has a compressed action characteristic of a console. Model 508 is the same as the 506, except with a fancier cabinet and assembled in North Carolina with an

Indonesian back. Model 606 is this piano in a furniture-style console and comes in two levels of cabinetry, the more expensive ones having inlayed veneers. Model K-18 is the 506 in a Japanese-style, polyester-finished cabinet. It replaces the recent CX-10 and its predecessor, the popular model CX-5H, as Kawai's low-priced "studio." The 46½" furniture-style studio model 902 has been changed to model 906, with a stiffer back structure, all ABS action parts, and new cabinetry. Model K-25 is like the 48" model K-30 (discontinued), except in a simpler cabinet. UST-10 and UST-12 are, respectively, 48" and 52" American-style institutional (school) uprights made in North Carolina with a Japanese back and action.

In the grands, the 5' model GM-2A has become model GM-10. The 5' 1" model GE-1A has been replaced by the GE-20, which has the features of the former GE-1AS model. A new 5' 5" model GE-30 has been introduced. It has the same scale as the model RX-1, but is like the other GE models structurally and in terms of its features (see *The Piano Book* for details on the differences between the RX, GE, and GM models).

Several of the grand and upright models are available in limited quantity in "Conservatory" and "Promotional" versions. The Conservatory models have a wider music rack than the regular models, usually larger or double casters and a lock, and sometimes cabinetry or aesthetics that are slightly simplified. Promotional models have a regular (not soft-fall) fallboard and some other simplified features. Prices were not available at press time, but are expected to be about the same or slightly less than regular models.

The Shigeru Kawai pianos are now available in six different models from 5' 10" to 9' 1".

KEMBLE

New U.S. distributor:

Poppenberg & Associates
966 South Pearl Street
Denver, Colorado 80209

303-765-5775

The "Cambridge" models have been discontinued. A new 46½" "Windsor" model has been added. This model has a fancier cabinet and a more powerful bass than the 45" "Traditional" model, also discontinued. The 52" vertical, formerly available only as a limited-edition designer model, is now available as a regular model. There is also a new Shaker-styled designer upright called "Vermont" designed by the famous British designers Conran and Partners, and a black polyester and chrome model called "Classic-T".

Kemble has introduced its first grand piano, a 5' 8" "Conservatoire" model, in cooperation with Yamaha, which owns a majority interest in Kemble. The grand is like the Yamaha model C2, with design differences such as plate color and music desk shape. It is also voiced to Kemble's specs, sounding to me more "European", i.e. a mellower bass.

KINGSBURG

This brand is now called Carl Ebel. See under "Perzina, Gebr."

KNABE, WM.

See under "Samick"

KRAKAUER

New e-mail address: daguillaume@earthlink.net

Change of phone number: 574-262-9952

MASON & HAMLIN

Mason & Hamlin is working on a new 6' 3" model AA grand, to be introduced in 2004.

MEISTER, OTTO

See "Beijing Xinghai"

MILLER, HENRY F. (new listing)

Henry F. Miller
236 West Portal Ave. #568
San Francisco, CA 94127

800-511-0083
info@henryfmiller.com

This is the name of an old American piano maker dating back to 1863, no longer in business. The name is now owned by the Sherman Clay chain of piano stores. Current Henry F. Miller pianos are made by Pearl River in

China and are similar to pianos sold under the Pearl River name. However, the company says in the future it may source these pianos from a variety of Asian manufacturers. The pianos are sold in Sherman Clay, Jordan Kitt's, and other major piano retailers throughout the country.

NORDISKA

Several new models include: a 43" model 109 continental-style console, a 48" model 118 console-styled upright, a 50" model 126 upright with six full-length spruce backposts and Abel hammers, among other features; and a 7' model 215 grand with maple rim and Renner action. This new grand had an especially good sound and touch, the best yet on a Chinese-made piano.

PEARL RIVER

New contact information for U.S. distributor:

Pearl River Piano Group America, Ltd.
2260 S. Haven Avenue, Suite F
Ontario, California 91761

909-673-9155
800-435-5086
usa@pearlriverpiano.com
www.pearlriverpiano.com

Pearl River has added 5' 7" and 6' 4" grands to its line. The company says these models are scaled to sound like Japanese or American pianos, whereas the other models are more European sounding. The 7' and 9' Pearl River grands now come with Renner actions.

A 49" vertical model 126R has been added to the Ritmüller line. The vertical is based on the model 125M1 joint venture piano (with Yamaha), but with agraffes throughout the scale.

Correction: The 4' 7" and 5' 3" Ritmüller grands do not come with Renner actions.

PERZINA, GEBR. (new listing)

Piano Empire, Inc.
13370 E. Firestone Blvd., Ste. A
Santa Fe Springs, CA 90670

800-576-3463
562-926-1906
info@kingsburgpiano.com
www.kingsburgpiano.com

Pianos made by: Yantai Longfeng Piano Co., Ltd., Yantai, China

Names used: Gebr. Perzina, Carl Ebel, Gerh. Steinberg, Kingsburg

The Gebr. Perzina piano company was established in the German town of Schwerin in 1871, and was a prominent piano maker until World War I, after which its fortunes declined. In more recent times, the factory was moved to the nearby city of Lenzen and the company is now known as Pianofabrik Lenzen GmbH. In the early 1990s, the company was purchased by Music Brokers International B.V. in The Netherlands. Eventually it was decided that making pianos in Germany was not economically viable, so manufacturing was moved to Yantai, China, where a range of verticals and grands are being made by the Yantai Longfeng Piano Co. under the Gebr. Perzina, Carl Ebel, and Gerh. Steinberg names. The Kingsburg name was also used until recently, but has been changed to Carl Ebel. (See also under "Kingsburg" in *The Piano Book*.)

The three brand names are all based on the same scale designs, but there are technical and cosmetic differences between them, with the Perzina brand positioned as highest quality, followed by the Steinberg and the Carl Ebel. The technical differences primarily involve the choice of action (Chinese, Czech, Japanese, German), hammers (English, Japanese, German), and soundboard taper (the Perzina grands have a tapered soundboard). In addition, the Perzina verticals have several interesting features rarely found in other pianos, including a "floating" soundboard which is unattached to the back at certain points for freer vibration, and a reverse, or concave, soundboard crown.

Lenzen says it ships many European materials to Yantai, including Roslau strings, Delignit pinblocks, English felts, and European veneers, as well as Alaskan Sitka spruce. New machinery is from Japan and Italy. According to the company, all the piano designs are the original German scales. The Renner actions used in some of the Perzina grands (models beginning with "E") are ordered complete from Germany, not assembled from German parts.

PETROF

Web site address: www.petrof.com

Petrof has introduced a new concert grand called the "P1 Mistral." The company says the instrument utilizes a more rigid brace and frame, front and rear duplex scales, and a Renner action, among other features. The Magnetic Balanced Action feature (see page 233 of *The Piano Book*) is available as an option. Also new is a 53" vertical model P135. It has a Renner action, full sostenuto, a soft-close fallboard, and a newly-designed adjustable music desk, among other features.

PIANODISC

PianoDisc has replaced the PDS 128 Plus system with the 228 CFX. The main difference is that the 228 CFX has both a floppy drive and a CD drive as standard equipment, so it is unnecessary to plug in your own CD player (although you can do so if you have a multi-disc CD changer you want to use). The company says that the control box is the smallest such box with both floppy and CD drives on the market. It can be mounted on the piano or can be located up to 100 feet away and operated with the included infrared wireless remote control.

PianoDisc has introduced an MX Platinum option that utilizes 64 MB of flash memory to store hours of music and play it back without ever having to change a disk. MX Platinum comes with 35 hours of pre-selected music (589 songs), to which one can add music from floppy disks, TFT MIDI Record, and standard MIDI files (but not PianoDisc CDs). PianoDisc's regular MX feature with 32 MB of flash memory still remains available as an option.

The GT360 and GT90 QuietTime systems have been discontinued and replaced with a QuietTime system that includes most of the same components, but without the sound card and control box. The new system comes with a power supply, MIDI cable, a MIDI strip for installing under the keys, three pedal switches, a MIDI board with cover, headphones, and a mute rail that, when activated, prevents the hammers from hitting the strings. Customers can buy and use any off-the-shelf sound module with the system.

A question often arises concerning the relationship of the PianoDisc system components to the QuietTime system. The answer is that if you purchase the PianoDisc playback system with the SymphonyPro Sound Module, the TFT MIDI Record system, and the PianoMute Rail, you have purchased virtually all the components of the QuietTime system and have therefore acquired the QuietTime system virtually "free." The separate listing for QuietTime in the price list is for those who wish to purchase it without the PianoDisc playback. Those people will need to purchase, in addition, a sound module from their music dealer.

PianoDisc has introduced a new remote control called the PianoDisc Home Theater Master. It features an LCD touch screen and eliminates the need to have multiple remote controls to operate other various electronic devices. This remote is specially programmed to operate the PianoDisc and can be programmed to control eleven other Audio and Video components including: Stereo, CD, Tape, CATV, Satellite, TV, DVD, VCR and Laser Disc.

Note Release Control (NRC) has been developed by PianoDisc to reduce noise made by the keys when they are released. This is achieved by pulsing the solenoid during key release to slow the key down. This new feature is compatible with all PDS 128+ and 228CFX Silent Drive systems, and is added by using the Flash Memory feature that allows for convenient software upgrades. To add NRC at no charge, get the PianoDisc Update 4.2 and Silent Drive CPU Update F from the PianoDisc web site or from an authorized PianoDisc installer.

For a limited time, PianoDisc is offering five hundred dollars in free music software with each PianoDisc system purchased. See your dealer for details.

The next generation PianoDisc system, Opus 7, is in development and is due to be released in 2004. It will feature a wireless, internet-ready, tablet PC as the system's "Conductor," with the ability to download music and system upgrades directly from PianoDisc's website, among other features.

PLEYEL

Pleyel pianos are now being distributed directly by the manufacturer:

Manufacture Francaise de Pianos
30319 Ales Cedex, France

(33) 4 66 56 25 00
pleyel.cial-france@wanadoo.fr
www.pleyel.fr

Pleyel has introduced a new 5' 8" model 170 grand piano.

PRAMBERGER

See "Young Chang"

QRS / PIANOMATION

QRS has made changes to its line of Pianomation player piano systems since publication of the Fourth Edition of *The Piano Book*. As mentioned in the book, Pianomation consists of a basic playback engine common to all its systems plus a choice of several different front-end controllers that determine the input to the system.

The simplest and least expensive controller is the model 2000C. The control box is hidden under the piano. It has no built-in disk drives, but instead uses your own off-the-shelf stereo components or computer to play MIDI files or QRS CDs and DVDs. The background music comes from your own stereo system, while a wireless transmitter sends the piano data to the Pianomation system, even through walls.

The model 2000CD+ is like the 2000C, above, but includes its own CD player for playing QRS audio CDs. It also comes with a speaker. Because of its "plug and play" simplicity, it is the easiest to use and most popular of the systems.

Formerly called "AMC" (Analog to MIDI Controller) and now called "Chili," this controller comes with both CD and floppy drives. The CD drive will play both audio CDs and data CDs (CD ROMs), the latter potentially containing thousands of MIDI files on a single CD. The company says this system will also play Yamaha Disklavier floppy disks, as well as Standard MIDI files type 1 and 0. It also has internal memory storage capabilities and comes with a record strip, a speaker, headphone outputs, and a sound module. Chili has both mixed and unmixed audio outputs so that the background music track and the piano track can be mixed for piping around the house, but the piano track can be omitted from the speakers located in the room containing the piano. Individual sources of audio sound can be finely adjusted so they will sound properly balanced at any volume level.

The above systems can be ordered or installed through any dealer doing business with QRS, but the company also makes two "Serenade" systems that are available only through an exclusive dealer network. Serenade CD is like the 2000CD+ system, but is only 1/2" high (for those who prefer their Pianomation to be as unobtrusive as possible) and plays both QRS audio CDs and PianoDisc CDs, according to the company. It comes with a remote control.

Serenade Pro is a fully-loaded system similar to Chili, with both floppy and CD (audio and CD ROM) drives, a sound module, record strip, and speaker, but also contains a hard drive (instead of internal memory) and a 900 mhz two-way wireless remote, has space for an optional karaoke card, and will play MP3 (live music) files. It does not have Chili's capability for both mixed and unmixed audio outputs and headphone jacks.

Sync-Along is a new feature that will play on either the Chili controller or the Serenade Pro. Similar to Yamaha's PianoSmart, QRS has prepared a piano track in MIDI format on a floppy disk to go along with each of a number of popular audio CDs and DVDs available on the general market. When the owner plays both the floppy and the CD or DVD at the same time, Sync-Along links them together, enabling Pianomation to accurately play along with the CD or DVD. A new Transcription series is similar to Sync-Along but without the background music or visual accompaniment. A solo performance audio CD or DVD is transcribed and offered as a QRS CD so the customer can hear the performance on his or her own piano.

The QRS record option used to be offered in both "LiteSwitch" and "OptiScan" versions. These have been discontinued. QRS is currently using the well-regarded Gulbransen record strip while it is developing a new generation of the OptiScan record system.

Apart from its player piano systems, QRS is constantly inventing new gadgets and gizmos for pianos that can be installed independently of Pianomation. Recent inventions include a Grand Mute Rail for quieting the sound of a grand piano (these have existed for verticals before, but not for grands), and a Grand Fallboard Closer that allows a grand fallboard to close gently and avoid hurting the player's fingers (available on many new pianos for some time, but not previously as an add-on accessory).

QRS has acquired the exclusive rights to manufacture and sell a Self-Tuning Piano System (which does not yet have a trade name). The company says the system will be designed into the manufacture of a piano and will allow the piano to maintain itself in tune between major tunings by a piano tuner. The system works by heating each string slightly to change its pitch. Initially the piano is tuned slightly sharp. While the system senses the pitch of each string, a tiny heating element under each string will heat it very slightly until it is lowered to the correct pitch. When the piano can no longer be tuned in this manner, it will need a regular tuning. It is expected that the system will be of particular interest to institutions. It was invented by Don A. Gilmore of Kansas City, Missouri.

RIDGEWOOD

The Ridgewood name is now applied to three models of piano from the Dongbei Piano Co., the model 112 (also called 110) vertical and the 5' and 5' 5" grands. All other Ridgewood models have been discontinued.

RIEGER-KLOSS

The Rieger-Kloss line of pianos has been discontinued. The Bohemia Piano Co. is now making and distributing pianos under its own name. See under "Bohemia" in this section for more information.

RITMÛLLER

See under "Pearl River"

SAGENHAFT

Use of the Sagenhaft name has been discontinued. Some of the same models are now sold under the Ridgewood name. See "Ridgewood."

SAMICK

New web site address: www.smcmusic.com

Samick Music Corporation, the North American marketing arm of the Korean company, is now known as SMC, and distributes Samick, Kohler & Campbell, Conover Cable, and Wm. Knabe pianos in North America. The company says it is also developing a line of Sohmer pianos (the name licensed from the owners of PianoDisc), but there is a trademark dispute over this name (see "Sohmer"). Under an arrangement with Baldwin, SMC is temporarily distributing Chickering pianos left over from a production run never claimed and paid for by Baldwin after its bankruptcy (see "Baldwin"). Samick has also recently acquired a majority interest in the C. Bechstein company, a major German manufacturer. See under "Bechstein, C." Samick is no longer making pianos under the Bernhard Steiner name.

The Wm. Knabe piano line made by Young Chang for PianoDisc has been discontinued, and PianoDisc has licensed the name to Samick. Samick is now using this name on the pianos formerly sold as the "World Piano" premium line of Samick pianos (see *The Piano Book* for details). Samick says plans are underway to make a new premium-level piano with the Knabe name based on the original nineteenth and early twentieth century Knabe scale designs and cabinet styles in use when the company was based in Baltimore, with sand-cast plates and lacquer finishes. At present, only the 6' 4" Knabe grand matches this description; a 5' 9" model is due in early 2004.

Samick has discontinued a number of models in its Samick, Kohler & Campbell, and Conover Cable lines and has come out with some new ones as well, both Korean and Indonesian. In general, it is continuing its trend of moving much of its production to Indonesia, while concentrating its Korean production on higher-end models. The company says its 4' 7" through 6' 1" grands will all soon be made in Indonesia, as well as all verticals except the Kohler & Campbell Millennium series uprights. K&C Millennium pianos, both grand and vertical, and all Sohmer and Knabe pianos are to be made in Korea.

For its higher-end pianos, Samick is now using what it calls a "Pratt Reed Premium Action." This is not to be confused with the Pratt-Read action used in many American-made pianos in the mid to late twentieth century and eventually acquired by Baldwin. Samick says its Pratt Reed action is made in Korea and designed after the German Renner action.

SAUTER

Additional web site address: www.sauter-pianos.de

SCHELL, LOTHAR (new listing)

Lothar Schell Musical Instruments
Shouda USA, Inc.
1224 Santa Anita Ave., Suite D
South El Monte, California 91733

888-707-4266
626-350-3800
shoudausa@yahoo.com

Lothar Schell is a German piano designer whose techniques and designs have been used in pianos throughout the world. The distributor prefers not to disclose where the pianos are made or how they might differ from other pianos made at the same factory, but says only that they are sourced from a variety of locations and that the specifications and materials are carefully chosen for quality by Mr. Schell. It would appear from the model listings that the present line of Lothar Schell grand pianos is made at the Dongbei piano factory in China.

SCHIMMEL

New address for U.S. distributor:

Schimmel Piano Corporation
577B Hackman Road
Lititz, Pennsylvania 17543

Schimmel has developed several new upright models based on a more traditional philosphy of construction. These are the F 122 (48"), S 125 (49"), and O 132 (52"). Older models in the same or similar sizes continue to be produced, however. In the older models, the plate is the main structural support and contains a pocket for the pinblock. In the new models, traditional back posts assume a greater role for support, and the pinblock and soundboard are attached to the posts. The company says that the joining of wooden structural and acoustical parts enhances the tone. The new models also incorporate duplex scaling.

Schimmel has released a new 5' 7" model 169 grand. The company says the piano has the same treble scale and action as its 7' grand, and almost the same size soundboard as its 6' grand. To obtain the larger soundboard, the case sides are angled slightly, a technique also now applied to all the grand models. The soundboard and ribs were also modified for tonal improvement. This philosophy of marrying the front end of the 7' grand to other sizes of piano is one that Schimmel plans to extend to other models as it creates a "family" of redesigned grands. An example of the new 5' 7" grand I played was typically bright, but had very good sustain and the feel of a larger piano. I was impressed with it. In 2003, Schimmel developed a new 6' 3" model 189 grand, presumably to replace the 6' model, though the latter is still available at this time. All the grands now have a similar sound and touch.

In 2002, Schimmel acquired the PianoEurope factory in Kalisz, Poland, a piano restoration facility and manufacturer of the Meyer piano brand, one not generally found in the U.S. Schimmel is using this factory to launch its "Vogel" brand, a less expensive line named after the company's co-president. Schimmel says that although the skill level of the employees is high, lower wages and other lower costs will result in a piano approximately thirty percent less costly than the Schimmel. Vogel pianos will feature Renner actions and other parts from Schimmel or local Polish suppliers. Schimmel says that some of the pianos may come into the U.S. with the Meyer name on them until the supply of those instruments is exhausted.

SCHUBERT

Although the focus these days is on the improvement in Chinese pianos, progress is also taking place in other parts of the world in which privatization and international joint ventures are underway. TRI-CON Music Group, which imports Schubert pianos from Belarus, has formed a joint venture with the Belarus factory that allows TRI-CON to control the quality of Belarus' production and make design changes, which it hopes will substantially improve quality. The company says improvements have already been made in virtually all areas, including materials, action geometry, finishes, and cabinet design. TRI-CON says it has its own quality-control personnel at the factory and that it will soon have control over all production and sales there. Sources tell me, however, that quality still lags behind most Chinese-made pianos.

SCHULZE POLLMANN

Schulze Pollmann has introduced a new 5' 3" model 160 grand. It comes with a Detoa action, but can be ordered with a Renner action at additional cost. The 46" model 117 vertical has a new scale design with agraffes and has been redesignated as model 118/P8. The 50" model 126E has been similarly redesigned and is now called 126P6.

SEILER

New U.S. contact information for Seiler:

888-621-1137
america@seiler-pianos.com
www.seiler-pianos.com

All Seiler grand models have been redesigned with a duplex scale, longer strings, larger soundboard area, longer keys, and a lighter touch. 5' 11" model 180 has become 6' 1" model 186; 6' 9" model 206 has become 6' 10" model 208; and 8' model 240 has become 8' model 242. I have had an opportunity to play models 208 and 242 (model 186 is brand new). Musically, both of these redesigned models are very successful. They retain the typical Seiler clarity, but with longer sustain and a marvelously even-feeling touch — a real pleasure to play.

Seiler has introduced its "Value Added Warranty." The warranty states that at the end of ten years from the date of purchase, a purchaser who has maintained his or her Seiler piano as required under the terms of the warranty may trade it in toward a new Seiler and receive a credit of the full original purchase price paid.

Seiler says that if there is no Seiler dealer in the customer's area, the customer can contact the U.S. representative to arrange for a direct purchase from Germany.

Correction: Seiler makes approximately 2,000 pianos a year.

SEJUNG (new listing)

America Sejung Corporation
295 Brea Canyon Road
Walnut, California 91789

909-839-0757
866-473-5864
sales@ASCpianos.com
www.ASCpianos.com

Pianos made by: Sejung Corp., Quingdao, China

Names used: Sejung, Falcone, Hobart M. Cable, Geo. Steck, Vivace

Sejung is a Korean-based textile, construction, and information technology business that was established in 1974, but the musical instrument portion of the business began only in 2001. In that year, the company's chairman received a proposal from an old friend with extensive experience in piano and guitar manufacturing to enter those businesses in a big way by manufacturing in China. Within a year, the company had partnered with a Chinese manufacturer (necessary for doing business in China); built a 700,000 square foot factory in Quingdao, a port city on the Eastern coast with a temperate climate; hired dozens of manufacturing managers who had once worked for Young Chang and Samick, and staffed the factory with some 2,000 workers, whom the company also feeds and houses in dormitories (necessary to attract good labor and reduce turnover). Although wages are incredibly low in China (less than one dollar per hour), the company says it has invested millions in automated production equipment in areas where precision counts, rather than just rely on cheap labor. The company produces just about every piano component in its own factories, and has a goal of producing 1,000 grand pianos and 2,000 verticals per month.

The first pianos from Sejung were shown in the U.S. in early 2003, less than one year after production began. I and other technicians examined a number of instruments at a trade show. Although still a little rough, they were definitely competent, and remarkably good for having been only an idea in someone's head less than two years earlier! The general consensus seems to be that Sejung will have little trouble bringing its quality up to that of the other Chinese manufacturers, and ahead of some, in a very short time, and is destined to be a major force in the world piano market.

For marketing the pianos in the U.S., Sejung has licensed the Falcone and Geo. Steck names from PianoDisc/Mason & Hamlin and the Hobart M.

Cable name from Story & Clark (see "Mason & Hamlin" and "Story & Clark" in *The Piano Book*). The name Vivace was used briefly but is being discontinued. Initially, the pianos are being sold primarily under the Falcone and Hobart M. Cable names, and the two lines are very similar. When use of the Geo. Steck name begins in early 2004, that and the Hobart M. Cable pianos will be similar (with some style differences) but the Falcone line will be upgraded in quality and features and will be priced about 20 percent higher than the other two.

For model and price information, see under "Falcone" and "Cable, Hobart M." in the Model and Pricing Guide section of this *Supplement*.

Warranty: The plate and pinblock are warranted to the original purchaser for as long as he or she owns the piano. The rest of the piano has a twelve year warranty on parts and ten years on labor. The warranty is not transferable.

SHERMAN CLAY

Correction: I have been told that for much of the 1970s and 1980s, pianos sold under the Sherman Clay label were made by Kimball or Aeolian. In the mid to late 1980s, some Sherman Clay pianos were made by Daewoo (Sojin).

SOHMER (& CO.)

Pianos are again being made under this venerable name, once considered among the finest of American-built instruments. However, there appears to be a dispute over the ownership of the Sohmer trademark, with pianos bearing this name being manufactured and distributed by two different companies.

SMC, distributor of Samick pianos, says it holds a license from the Burgett brothers, owners of PianoDisc, to use the Sohmer name. The Burgetts acquired the Sohmer trademark registrations when they purchased the assets of Mason & Hamlin out of bankruptcy in 1996. A distributor doing business under the name Persis International, Inc., who applied for the Sohmer trademark in 2001, claims that the registrations acquired by the Burgetts are expired, that the trademark had been legally abandoned by not being used since the 1994 closing of the Sohmer factory in Pennsylvania, and that the Burgetts' application to re-register was refused. SMC and the Burgetts argue that the Sohmer trademark has been in almost continuous use for more than 130 years, that the Burgetts never had any intention of abandoning it and have proof that they did not abandon it, and that the government erred in canceling its prior registration and in not approving its new application.

Documents received from the U.S. Patent and Trademark Office confirm that the government considers all past registrations of the Sohmer trademark to be expired or canceled and that the Burgetts' new application was refused, subject to appeal. Further action on Persis' application has been temporarily suspended pending the Burgetts' appeal. At press time, the application process was still ongoing and it may be some time before the issue is settled for good. In the meantime, piano shoppers may find two "Sohmer" pianos in the marketplace. (Note: Persis' pianos are labeled "Sohmer" and SMC's are labeled "Sohmer & Co.") Both companies submitted product information, including model and price data, for this *Supplement*.

Persis International, Inc.
3540 N. Southport #116
Chicago, Illinois 60657

800-445-0695

Sohmer pianos from this distributor are manufactured by Royale, a Korean firm that is descended from the now-defunct joint venture between Ibach and Daewoo (see "Ibach"). Models include a 50" vertical and 5' 3", 5' 10", and 7' 2" grands. The distributor says the pianos have high quality components, such as Renner actions, Abel hammers, Delignit pinblocks, and Ciresa soundboards.

SMC
18521 Railroad St.
City of Industry, California 91748

800-592-9393
626-964-4700
www.smcmusic.com

Sohmer & Co. pianos from this distributor will be made in Korea by Samick. The Sohmer & Co. model 34, a 42" vertical, will feature full-length backposts, a sand-cast plate, exposed 16-ply pinblock, and a slow-close fallboard—virtually identical (except for the slow-close fallboard) to the original, highly regarded Sohmer & Co. console. Sohmer & Co. grands will be based on the pianos Samick made for Baldwin under the Chickering label. They will have maple outer rims, sand-cast plates, spruce beams, solid brass hardware, agraffes, and other higher quality features. In 2004, SMC plans to introduce a 45" Sohmer & Co. piano based on a Bechstein vertical scale, but with original Sohmer & Co. styling.

STECK, GEO.

PianoDisc has discontinued its Geo. Steck line of PianoDisc-equipped, Chinese-made pianos. The name has been licensed to new Chinese manufacturer Sejung, but is not yet in use at press time. See "Sejung".

STEINBERG, GERH.

See "Perzina, Gebr."

STEINBERG, WILH.

The name of the manufacturer has changed from Wilhelm Steinberg Pianofortefabrik Gmbh to Thüringer Pianoforte GmbH. The company has also sold its key-making business to Kluge, now part of Steinway.

Steinberg says it will not be making the 49" vertical available with a Fandrich action, as mentioned in *The Piano Book*.

The warranty has been changed to five years, parts and labor.

Although not rated in *The Piano Book*, Wilh. Steinberg pianos, both grand and vertical, are well made and would probably be rated in Group 2.

Correction: *The Piano Book* says that the Wilh. Steinberg grand is identical to the Steingraeber grand. Although the Steinberg grand evolved from the Steingraeber, unlike the Steingraeber, the Steinberg has a duplex scale, as well as a different method of rim construction and a different bridge design.

"Eisenberg" is a new, lower-priced line from Steinberg, made in cooperation with other European factories. Eisenberg will start shipping in fall of 2003. The former 48" Steinberg model C2, with a simpler cabinet and a different soundboard than the other Steinberg models, is expected to be part of the new line. At press time, prices and models were not yet firm.

STEINER, BERNHARD

Samick is no longer making pianos under this name.

STEINGRAEBER & SÖHNE

Additional web site address: www.steingraeber.de

Steingraeber has a new 8' 9" concert grand, model E-272 (price not available).

Steingraeber is known for its many innovative technical improvements to the piano. The newest one is a cylindrical knuckle (grand piano part) that revolves when played softly. It acts like a normal knuckle during normal and hard playing, but the revolving knuckle makes pianissimo playing easier, smoother, and more accurate.

STEINLAGER (new listing)

A-440 Pianos
4100 Steve Reynolds Blvd., Suite F
Norcross, Georgia 30093

770-717-8047
888-565-5648

pianomen@earthlink.net
www.A440pianos.com

Steinlager pianos are made in China by Sejung (see "Sejung") and are similar to Sejung's Falcone and Hobart M. Cable pianos.

STEINWAY & SONS

Steinway has launched its new Legendary Collection—one-of-a-kind reproductions of historical art case pianos—with a reproduction of the famous Alma Tadema art case Steinway. Commissioned in the 1880s by Henry Marquand, then-president of the Metropolitan Museum of Art in New York, this piano was designed and created by the famous English design firm of Sir Lawrence Alma-Tadema. In 1997, it was purchased at Sotheby's for $1,200,000. Offered at a price of $675,000, the reproduction, like the original, contains just about every possible art case decoration possible, including elaborate carvings, 17 different levels of decorative moldings, medallions, engravings, inlaid mother-of-pearl, marquetry, goatskin parchment, a frieze consisting of more than 6,000 parts, and even an oil painting. It is considered the most expensive piano ever built.

As mentioned in *The Piano Book*, Steinway has made small design changes to its vertical pianos to make them easier to tune, including shortening the tuning pin length, reducing string bearing angles, correcting alignment problems in the plate, and adding string-stretching operations at the factory. Some technicians report that the vertical pianos now tune with the same ease as other brands.

This year Steinway commemorates its 150th anniversary with numerous events, concerts, publications, and several new art case pianos.

Correction: On page 206 of *The Piano Book*, I wrote that Steinway operated its own plate foundry until about 1930. My sources now tell me that the foundry operated until about 1939 or 1940.

STORY & CLARK

Web site address: www.storyandclark.com

In part due to economic factors and in part because of the problems of Baldwin, a principal supplier of parts, Story & Clark has ceased all its U.S. piano production. Pianos bearing the Story & Clark name are now made in China by the Dongbei piano factory, except for the largest upright, which is made by Beijing.

STRAUSS

New distributor contact information:

L & M International, Inc.
5601 Ottershaw Ct.
Brentwood, Tennessee 37027

615-309-9285
www.strausspiano.com

A new 46½" model UP-118 vertical I saw at a trade show sounded, played, and looked much better than previous models I have seen from this company.

The company now provides a ten year limited parts and labor warranty from the manufacturer.

SUZUKI (new listing)

Suzuki Corporation
P.O. Box 261030
San Diego, California 92196

800-854-1594
858-566-9710
www.suzukimusic.com

Suzuki Corporation, the world's largest producer of musical instruments for education, and a household word in music education, has entered the acoustic piano business with a line of verticals and grands made in China by Dongbei. The pianos feature solid spruce soundboards, German Delignit pinblocks, and German Roslau strings.

VOGEL

See "Schimmel"

WALTER, CHARLES R.

New phone number (area code change): 574-266-0615

Web site address: www.walterpiano.com

Walter says he has made some changes to his vertical pianos to better control tuning pin torque (tightness), to reduce the incidence of false beats in the treble, and to smooth out the break between tenor and bass.

Release of a 5' 8" grand is scheduled for late 2003.

WEBER

Weber has introduced a number of "special edition" grand and vertical models. The "WSG" grand models—5' 7", and 6' 1"—have tapered soundboards, "best quality" Young Chang actions, and cosmetic enhancements. The "WSE" 48" verticals have cosmetic and action enhancements.

Weber has added two more Chinese-made grands to its line, 5' 2" and 5' 9". These are made in Young Chang's Tianjin factory.

Behning is a new line of pianos distributed by Weber. They are made in China by Sejung (see "Sejung").

WHELPDALE, MAXWELL & CODD

This company was renamed The British Piano Manufacturing Company Ltd. See under that name for more information. The company ceased operations in April 2003.

WOODCHESTER

Woodchester was purchased by Whelpdale, Maxwell & Codd, later called The British Piano Manufacturing Company Ltd., which ceased operations in April 2003. See under "British" for more information.

WYMAN (new listing)

Wyman Piano Company LLC
P.O. Box 218802
Nashville, Tennessee 37221

615-356-9143
info@wymanpiano.com
www.wymanpiano.com

Wyman Piano Company is a new venture created by experienced former Baldwin executives. The Wyman line consists of six vertical piano sizes (including a 39" 73-note model) and four grand sizes in a variety of cabinet styles and finishes. All are manufactured in China by the Beijing Xinghai Piano Company (see "Beijing Xinghai"). The verticals are probably similar to the ones made by Beijing under the Ellington name and sold by Baldwin, but with cabinetry differences (see "Baldwin"). Wyman says that its executives make frequent trips to Beijing to monitor manufacturing and inspect finished instruments. The pianos come with a ten-year parts and labor warranty.

XINGHAI

See "Beijing Xinghai"

YAMAHA
including Disklavier

Yamaha has replaced its 4' 11" model GA1 grand and corresponding Disklavier model DGA1 with less expensive, Indonesian-made versions, models GA1E and DGA1E, respectively.

Perhaps in response to criticisms of the tone of its 5' 3" GH1B series of grands (or perhaps because the introduction of an inexpensive piano from Indonesia has made the low-priced 5' 3" pianos redundant), Yamaha has replaced the GH1B series, and the less-expensive variant model GP1, with a new 5' 3" GC1 series. The new models feature the same scale design, duplex scaling, and tone collector construction as the more expensive C1 series, but with a bass sustain pedal instead of a sostenuto, and with less expensive cabinetry and plate finish. The price of the GC1 is about the same as the GH1B and it is available in most of the same furniture styles and finishes. A Disklavier version of the GC1, the DGC1A, replaces the corresponding Disklavier versions of the GH1B and GP1 pianos being discontinued.

Grand model C3 and its Disklavier counterpart DC3A are now available in a "NEO" cabinet style—a modernistic case with an acrylic lid, silver plate, and cherry legs. The model C1 "Metro" and its Disklavier counterpart are special centennial edition pianos with a unique rim design in polished ebony and champagne gold. They mark the 100th anniversary of the first Yamaha grand.

Model M475 is a new 44" console with cabinetry sophistication halfway between models M450 and M500. Fancy furniture versions of the popular P22 studio are now offered as model P600. Upright models U1 and U3 now sport a longer music desk—a very welcome addition. Model U3 joins model U5 in the use of a "floating" soundboard support system—the soundboard is not completely attached to the back at the top, allowing it to vibrate a little more freely for enhanced tonal performance.

The "A" at the end of most Disklavier model designations refers to the new CD (audio) function in these instruments, one of the Mark III (i.e., third generation) Disklavier features. Disklavier grands are no longer available without the CD function, except for model DGA1E and DGC1. Most Disklavier verticals don't have the CD function; however, it can be added. DCD1 is an add-on CD drive that can be added to any Disklavier grand or vertical, new or old.

The model DU1A is a new Disklavier version of the 48" U1 upright. It is the only Disklavier upright with Mark III features. It replaces both the MX1Z Disklavier and the MPX1Z Disklavier with Silent Feature. The DU1A contains the Silent Feature; a version of this model without the Silent Feature is no longer offered. The 48" MIDIPiano model MP1Z will become the MPU1.

Disklavier Pro models now have all the Mark III Disklavier features (except built-in speakers), including the CD drive, 16 MB of flash memory, and SmartKey and CueTime.

PianoSmart technology is a new feature of all Mark III Disklavier pianos. Yamaha has prepared a piano track in MIDI format on a floppy disk to go along with each of a number of popular audio CDs available on the general market. When the owner plays both the floppy and the CD at the same time, PianoSmart links them together, enabling the Disklavier to accurately play along with the CD. One can also record a piano accompaniment to a favorite audio CD. Pop the CD and a blank floppy into a Mark III Disklavier and record yourself playing along. The two will then be linked together for future playback. PianoSmart is available as a free software upgrade from Yamaha. The "smart" MIDI files will be added to the library of Disklavier musical offerings available from Yamaha. Customers with older Disklavier versions can retrofit PianoSmart into their system by buying the DCD1 Disklavier CD player and a software upgrade, although it may require a memory upgrade as well.

YOUNG CHANG
including Bergmann and Pramberger

Young Chang America has changed its corporate name to A N D Music Corporation.

In *The Piano Book*, I stated that Young Chang was retiring its "Gold" series in favor of its Pramberger Signature series. The Gold series has now been resurrected as Young Chang's upper-level Chinese line from its factory in Tianjin, China. Model numbers begin with "G". It differs from the company's Bergmann line (also made in China) as follows: Warranty (twelve years on Young Chang "Gold", ten years on Bergmann); cosmetic differences in legs, casters, plate color, inner rim color, lid, other cabinetry; tapered soundboard and upgraded hammers on Young Chang "Gold" grands; laminated soundboard on Bergmann verticals, solid spruce soundboard on Young Chang "Gold" verticals.

All Bergmann model numbers now begin with "B," the grands with "BTG." A new 5' 9" model BTG-175 and 6' 1" model BTG-185, both made in China, are based on the scales of the corresponding Young Chang "Gold" series pianos.

Young Chang says it has changed the front duplex scale on all its grand models to a new configuration for a cleaner sound.

Additions to the Pramberger "Platinum Edition" series now includes a 52" model JP-52 upright and a 7' 6" model JP-228 grand. Beginning in 2003, all Pramberger grands come with a Pramberger/Renner action (Renner parts on a Pramberger action frame), including the damper action. These actions can be identified by their wooden action rail and the Renner label.

The Kurzweil Player System (KPS) is similar to the QRS Chili system when installed in Young Chang pianos. When installed in Bergmann pianos, the KPS is only available as the QRS 2000 CD + system.

MODEL and PRICING GUIDE

This guide contains the "list price" for nearly every brand, model, style, and finish of new piano that has regular distribution in the United States and, for the most part, Canada. Some marginal, local, or "stencil" brands are omitted. Except where indicated, prices are in U.S. dollars and the pianos are assumed to be for sale in the U.S. (Canadians will find the information useful after translation into Canadian dollars, but there may be differences in import duties and sales practices that will affect retail prices.) Prices and specifications are, of course, subject to change. Most manufacturers revise their prices at least once a year; two or three times a year is not uncommon when currency exchange rates are unstable. The prices in this edition were compiled in the spring of 2003.

During the past year, the U.S. Dollar has dropped in value against the Euro by at least twenty percent. This has the potential effect of making European products twenty percent more expensive in the U.S., though in practice manufacturers may absorb some of that increase by cutting costs or accepting reduced profits. Some price increases are already reflected in this *Supplement*; other may occur later in the year.

Some terms used in this guide require special explanation and disclaimers:

List Price

The list price is usually a starting point for negotiation, not a final sales price. The term "list price," as used in this *Supplement*, is a "standard" or "normalized" list price computed from the published wholesale price according to a formula commonly used in the industry. Some manufacturers use a different formula, however, for their own suggested retail prices, usually one that raises the prices above "standard" list by ten to fifteen percent so that their dealers can advertise a larger "discount" without losing profit. For this reason, price-shopping by comparing discounts from the manufacturers' own suggested retail prices may result in a faulty price comparison. To provide a level playing field for comparing prices, all prices in this guide are computed according to a uniform "standard" formula, *even though it may differ from the manufacturers' own suggested retail prices.* Where my list prices and those of a manufacturer differ, then, no dishonesty should be inferred; we simply employ different formulas. For most brands, but not all, the price includes a bench and the standard manufacturer's warranty for that brand (see *The Piano Book* for details). Prices for some European brands do not include a bench. Most dealers will also include moving and one or two tunings in the home, but these are optional and a matter of agreement between you and the dealer.

Style and Finish

Unless otherwise indicated, the cabinet style is assumed to be "traditional" and is not stated. Exactly what "traditional" means varies from brand to brand. In general, it is a "classic" styling with minimal embellishment and straight legs. The vertical pianos have front legs, which are free-standing on smaller verticals and attached to the cabinet with toe blocks on larger verticals. "Continental" or European styling refers to vertical pianos without decorative trim and usually without front legs. Other furniture styles (Chippendale, French Provincial, Queen Anne, etc.) are as noted. The manufacturer's own trademarked style name is used when an appropriate generic name could not be determined.

Unless otherwise stated, all finishes are assumed to be "satin," which reflects light but not images. "Polished" finishes, also known as "high-gloss" or "high-polish," are mirror-like. "Oiled" finishes are usually matte (not shiny). "Open-pore" finishes, common on some European pianos, are slightly "grainier" satin finishes due to the wood pores not being filled in prior to finishing. In fact, many finishes labeled "satin" on European pianos are actually open-pore. "Ebony" is a black finish.

Special-order–only styles and finishes are in italics.

Some descriptions of style and finish may be slightly different from the manufacturer's own for the purpose of clarity, consistency, saving space, or other reason.

Size

The height of a vertical piano is measured from the floor to the top of the piano. The length of a grand piano is measured from the very front (keyboard end) to the very back (tail end).

About Actual Selling or "Street" Prices

Buying a piano is something like buying a car—the list price is deliberately set high in anticipation of negotiating.[*]   But sometimes this is carried to extremes, as when the salesperson reduces the price three times in the first fifteen minutes to barely half the sticker price. In situations like this, the customer, understandably confused, is bound to ask in exasperation, "What is the *real* price of this piano?"

Unfortunately, there *is* no "real" price. In theory, the dealer pays a wholesale price and then marks it up by an amount sufficient to cover the overhead and produce a profit. In practice, however, the markup can vary considerably from sale to sale depending on such factors as:

- how long the inventory has been sitting around, racking up finance charges for the dealer

- how much of a discount the dealer received at the wholesale level for buying in quantity or for paying cash

- the dealer's cash flow situation

- the competition in that particular geographic area for a particular brand or type of piano

- special piano sales events taking place in the area

- how the salesperson sizes up your situation and your willingness to pay

- the level of pre- and post-sale service the dealer seeks to provide

- the dealer's other overhead expenses

It's not unusual for one person to pay fifty percent more than another for the same brand and model of piano—sometimes even from the same dealer on the same day! It may seem as if pricing is so chaotic that no advice can be given, but in truth, enough piano sales do fall within a certain range of typical profit margins that some guidance is possible as long as the reader understands the limitations inherent in this kind of advice.

Historically, discounts from "standard" list price have averaged ten or fifteen percent in the piano business. In recent years, however, conditions

---

[*] A relatively small number of dealers have non-negotiable prices.

have changed such that, according to some industry sources, the average discount from list has increased to twenty or twenty-five percent. Essentially, due to growing competition from used pianos and digital pianos, and a decrease in the cultural importance attached to having a piano in the home, there are too many dealers of new pianos chasing after too few consumer dollars. In addition, higher labor costs worldwide and unfavorable international currency values make some brands so expensive in the U.S. that they can only be sold at very large discounts. I think, too, that consumers are becoming more savvy and are shopping around. Unfortunately, the overhead costs of running a traditional piano store are so high that most dealers cannot stay in business if they sell at an average discount from "standard" list price of more than about twenty percent. To survive, dealers are evolving multiple new approaches: becoming more efficient, instituting low-price/high volume strategies, cutting their overhead—sometimes including service—or subsidizing their meager sales of new pianos with used pianos (which command higher profit margins), rentals, rebuilding, and other products and services.

Although the average discount has increased, it is by no means uniform. Some brands dependably bring top dollar; others languish or the price is highly situational. I did consider giving a typical range of "street" prices for each brand and model listed in this volume, but concluded that the task would be too daunting due to the extreme variation that can exist from one situation to another, and because of the political fallout that would likely result from dealers and manufacturers who fear the loss of what little power they still have over aggressive, price-shopping customers. So, for now, I've decided just to give general advice in print. (For those who desire more specific information on "street" prices, I offer additional services, such as private telephone consultations and a Pricing Guide Service on the internet. See my web site, **www.pianobook.com**, for more information.)

One way some manufacturers assist dealers in overcoming downward price pressure is to publish wholesale price lists that are less than honest. That is, dealers are routinely offered large discounts (ten percent or more) from the published wholesale price if they buy in sufficient quantity, or for certain models, or for any other reason the manufacturer can think of. Since the prices in this *Supplement* are calculated from the published wholesale prices, this practice results in over-inflated list prices in this book for those particular companies, allowing dealers of those brands to advertise larger "discounts" without losing profit. This practice is especially common among some Chinese and Korean companies, but seems to be spreading. (Most manufacturers offer small discounts from the published wholesale price list from time to time or for paying cash, but lately some manufacturers seem to be carrying this practice to greater heights.) The problem for the consumer is that these wholesale discounts are not given out uniformly by manufacturers or among dealers, another reason why an appropriate "street" price figured from the price information presented here will have to remain a rough estimate.

It should be clearly understood that the advice given here is based on my own observations, subjective judgment, and general understanding of the piano market, *not* on statistical sales data or scientific analysis. (Brand-by-brand statistical sales data are virtually nonexistent.) This knowledge is the product of discussions with hundreds of customers, dealers, technicians, and industry executives over the years. Other industry observers may come to different conclusions. This rundown of "street" prices won't cover every brand, but should give a rough idea of what to expect and the ability to predict prices for some of the brands not specifically covered. I can't emphasize enough, however, that pricing can be highly situational, dependent on the mix of available products and the ease of comparison shopping in any particular geographic area, as well as on the financial situation of dealer and customer. The following generalizations should prove useful to you, but expect almost anything.

As a general rule of thumb:

- the more expensive the piano, the higher the possible discount

- the more "exclusive" a brand is perceived to be, the less likely head-to-head competition, and therefore the lower the possible discount

- the longer a piano remains unsold, the higher the possible discount

- the more service-intensive the piano, the lower the possible discount

Although discounts from "standard" list price for most Asian pianos typically start at perhaps fifteen percent, twenty or even thirty percent discounts are not uncommon in a moderately competitive environment, especially if the dealer knows the customer is shopping around. Both Chinese and Korean pianos are disadvantaged by the presence in the market of too many different brand names made by the same few companies, driving prices down. On the other hand, Chinese pianos are so inexpensive, and some still require so much servicing by the dealer, that it's simply not cost-effective to sell them for much less than full list price. So dealers often just use them as "loss leaders," that is, just to get people into the store, whereupon the customer is sold on a more expensive piano.

The Boston piano, although manufactured in Japan, is generally viewed as being a little more "exclusive" due to its association with Steinway, so deep discounting is much less likely. Discounts in the range of ten percent or so are common. Baldwin, whose pianos are usually seen as being distinctly different from the Asian products even though they often share common price ranges, also benefits from exceptional name recognition and its historical "made in USA" connection. Discounting is likely to be moderate, in my experience—perhaps fifteen to twenty-five percent. (Note: Due to Baldwin's recent bankruptcy and sale, however, discounting has tended to be larger than usual during the past couple of years. Until this situation settles down, some very large discounts may be possible on Baldwin products in selected situations.)

Western European instruments tend to be extremely expensive here due to their high quality, the high European cost of doing business, additional middlemen/importers and, sometimes, unfavorable exchange rates. There appear to be two types of dealers of these pianos. One type, specializing in selling higher-quality instruments to a demanding clientele, manages to get top dollar for them despite their high price, with discounts averaging only twenty percent or so. They are not particularly into negotiating. The other type of dealer, probably more numerous, depends for his or her "bread and butter" on consumer-grade pianos and is pleased to make a relatively small profit on the occasional sale of a luxury instrument. Discounts here may well approach thirty to forty percent at times, especially if the piano has gone unsold for an extended period of time. Eastern European brands like Petrof and Estonia are already seen as being a good deal for the money, so expect moderate discounts—perhaps fifteen to twenty-five percent.

Steinway pianos have always been in a class by themselves, historically the only expensive piano to continually command high profit margins. Except for older Steinways and the occasional Mason & Hamlin, Steinway has little competition and fewer than one hundred dealers in the United States. Service requirements can be quite high, at least in part because of the higher standards often required to satisfy a fussier clientele. Historically, Steinway pianos have sold at or near full list price. (Some dealers even sell *above* list!) This is still true in many places, but in recent years I have seen a little more discounting than in the past. Ten to fifteen percent is not unusual in some areas; as much as twenty percent would be rare.

For brands not mentioned or implied in the above discussion, it's usually a safe bet to figure a discount of fifteen to twenty-five percent from the prices in this *Supplement*, with greater discounts possible in selected situations.

There is no "fair" price for a piano except the one the buyer and seller agree on. The dealer is no more obligated to sell you a piano at a deep discount than you are obligated to pay the list price. Many dealers are simply not able to sell at the low end of the range consistently and still stay in business. It's understandable that you would like to pay the lowest price possible, and there's no harm in asking, but remember that piano shopping is not just about chasing the lowest price. Be sure you are getting the instrument that best suits your needs and preferences and that the dealer is committed to providing the proper pre- and post-sale service.

(Note: Remember that the "street" price discounts suggested above should be subtracted from the "standard" list prices in this *Supplement*, not from the manufacturer's suggested retail price.)

For more information on shopping for a new piano and on how to save money, please see pages 60–75 in *The Piano Book* (fourth edition).

Albrecht, Charles

Verticals

Model	Size	Style and Finish	Price*
4300	43"	Contemporary Polished Ebony	4,695.
4300	43"	Contemporary Polished Mahogany	4,795.
4300	43"	Contemporary Walnut	4,395.
4300	43"	Contemporary Polished Walnut	4,795.
4300	43"	Contemporary Cherry	4,395.
4300	43"	Contemporary Polished Ivory	4,795.
4300	43"	Contemporary Polished White	4,795.
4401	44"	Designer Cherry	5,395.
4401	44"	Designer Mahogany	5,395.
4403	44"	Designer Cherry	5,395.
4403	44"	Designer Brown Oak	5,395.
4406	44"	Designer Brown Oak	5,295.
4413	44"	Designer Cherry	6,895.
4413	44"	Designer Walnut	6,695.
4507	45"	Institutional Cherry	4,795.
4507	45"	Institutional Walnut	4,795.
4507	45"	Institutional Polished Ivory	4,995.
4507	45"	Institutional Polished White	4,995.
4517	45"	Designer Polished Ebony	6,495.
4517	45"	Designer Polished Mahogany	6,995.
4517	45"	Designer Polished Walnut	6,995.
4701	47"	Designer Cherry	5,895.
4701	47"	Designer Mahogany	5,895.
4703	47"	Designer Cherry	5,895.
4703	47"	Designer Mahogany	5,895.
4706	47"	Designer Brown Oak	5,595.
4803	48"	Institutional Polished Ebony	5,995.
4803	48"	Institutional Polished Mahogany	6,395.
4907	49"	Institutional Polished Ebony	6,295.
4907	49"	Institutional Polished Mahogany	6,695.
4907	49"	Institutional Polished Walnut	6,695.
5207	52"	Institutional Ebony or Polished Ebony	7,595.
5207	52"	Institutional Polished Mahogany	7,995.
5207	52"	Institutional Polished Walnut	7,995.
5207	52"	Institutional Polished Ivory	7,595.

*For explanation of terms and prices, please see pages 42–48.

Albrecht, Charles (continued)

Grands

Model	Size	Style and Finish	Price*
G4801	4' 8"	"Petite" Polished Ebony	12,595.
G4801	4' 8"	"Petite" Polished Mahogany	13,695.
G4801	4' 8"	"Petite" Polished Walnut	13,695.
G4801	4' 8"	"Petite" Polished White	12,995.
G5309	5' 3-1/2"	Polished Ebony	14,495.
G5309	5' 3-1/2"	Polished Mahogany	14,995.
G5309	5' 3-1/2"	Polished Walnut	14,995.
G5701	5' 7"	Ebony and Polished Ebony	16,395.
G5701	5' 7"	Polished Mahogany	16,995.
G5701	5' 7"	Polished Walnut	16,995.
G5701	5' 7"	Polished White	16,395.
G6101	6' 1"	Ebony and Polished Ebony	17,395.
G6101	6' 1"	Polished Mahogany	17,995.
G6101	6' 1"	Polished Walnut	17,995.

Astin-Weight

Verticals

Model	Size	Style and Finish	Price*
375	41"	Santa Fe Oiled Oak	8,740.
375	41"	Spanish Oiled Oak	7,980.
375	41"	Spanish Lacquer Oak	8,180.
375	41"	Italian Oiled Walnut	8,380.
375	41"	Italian Lacquer Walnut	8,580.
375	41"	Regency Oiled Oak	8,380.
375	41"	Regency Lacquer Oak	8,500.
375	41"	Regency Oiled Walnut	8,500.
375	41"	Regency Lacquer Walnut	8,520.
U-500	50"	Oiled Oak	13,380.
U-500	50"	Santa Fe Oiled Oak	14,780.
U-500	50"	Lacquer Oak	13,780.
U-500	50"	Oiled Walnut	13,980.
U-500	50"	Lacquer Walnut	14,380.

Grands

Model	Size	Style and Finish	Price*
———	5' 9"	Ebony	35,700.

Model	Size	Style and Finish	Price*

August Förster — see "Förster, August"

Baldwin

Verticals

Model	Size	Style and Finish	Price*
660E	43-1/2"	Georgian Mahogany	5,400.
662E	43-1/2"	Queen Anne Regency Cherry	5,400.
665E	43-1/2"	Transitional Country Oak	5,400.
667E	43-1/2"	Country French Oak	5,400.
2090E	43-1/2"	Hepplewhite Vintage Mahogany	6,320.
2095E	43-1/2"	Regal Oak	6,320.
2096E	43-1/2"	Queen Anne Royal Cherry	6,320.
243E	45"	Ebony	6,660.
243E	45"	Golden Oak	6,410.
243E	45"	American Walnut	6,660.
5050E	45"	Limited Edition Chippendale Mahogany	9,660.
5052E	45"	Limited Edition Queen Anne Cherry	9,660.
5057E	45"	Limited Edition Georgian Oak	9,660.
5062E	45"	Lim. Ed. Queen Anne Distressed Cherry	9,660.
248E	48"	Polished Ebony	9,550.
248E	48"	American Walnut	9,550.
6000E	52"	Ebony	12,350.
6000E	52"	Mahogany	12,650.
6000E	52"	Regency Cherry with Gold Trim	13,950.

Grands

Model	Size	Style and Finish	Price*
M1	5' 2"	Ebony	30,120.
M1	5' 2"	Polished Ebony	31,310.
M1	5' 2"	Mahogany	31,200.
M1	5' 2"	Polished Mahogany	33,530.
M1	5' 2"	Walnut	32,030.
M1	5' 2"	Polished Walnut	33,930.
M1	5' 2"	Polished Cherry	33,170.
225E	5' 2"	French Provincial Cherry	37,860.
R1	5' 8"	Ebony	33,890.
R1	5' 8"	Polished Ebony	35,280.
R1	5' 8"	Mahogany	35,340.
R1	5' 8"	Polished Mahogany	37,680.

*For explanation of terms and prices, please see pages 42–48.

Baldwin (continued)

Model	Size	Style and Finish	Price*
R1	5' 8"	Walnut	36,310.
R1	5' 8"	Polished Walnut	38,480.
R1	5' 8"	Polished Cherry	37,590.
R1	5' 8"	Polished Bubinga	43,730.
R1	5' 8"	Polished Rosewood	47,100.
R1	5' 8"	Polished Pommele	47,100.
226E	5' 8"	French Provincial Cherry	41,760.
226E	5' 8"	French Provincial Polished Cherry	43,190.
227E	5' 8"	Louis XVI Mahogany	41,760.
L1	6' 3"	Ebony	38,260.
L1	6' 3"	Polished Ebony	39,700.
L1	6' 3"	Mahogany	39,830.
L1	6' 3"	Polished Mahogany	42,230.
L1	6' 3"	Walnut	41,040.
L1	6' 3"	Polished Walnut	43,510.
L1	6' 3"	Polished Cherry	42,390.
SF10E	7'	Ebony	53,800.
SF10E	7'	Polished Ebony	55,550.
SF10E	7'	Mahogany	55,550.
SD10	9'	Ebony	86,030.
SD10	9'	Polished Ebony	86,070.

ConcertMaster (approximate, including installation by factory or dealer)

Verticals	Playback only / with Perf. Option	9,560./10,920.
Grands	Playback only / with Perf. Option	10,320./11,780.
	With stop rail, add $450	

Note: Discounts may apply, especially as an incentive to purchase the piano.

Bechstein, C.

Note: Some models say "C. Bechstein," others say only "Bechstein." See article in Manufacturer and Product Update section of this Supplement for details.

Verticals

Model	Size	Style and Finish	Price*
Balance	45-1/2"	Polished Ebony	23,024.
Avance	46-1/2"	Polished Ebony	26,704.
Ars Nova	49"	Polished Ebony	32,086.

Model	Size	Style and Finish	Price*
Concert 8	52"	Polished Ebony	41,516.
Concert 8	52"	Polished Mahogany	44,276.
Concert 8	52"	*Add for sostenuto*	3,910.
Grands			
160	5' 3"	Polished Ebony (Fall 2003)	44,850.
160	5' 3"	Polished Mahogany (Fall 2003)	47,150.
160	5' 3"	Specialty Woods (Fall 2003)	54,970.
160	5' 3"	*With Inlays, add"l*	7,338.
160	5' 3"	*With Classic Styling, add'l*	4,532.
180	5' 11"	Polished Ebony (Jan. 2004)	47,380.
180	5' 11"	Polished Mahogany (Jan. 2004)	49,680.
180	5' 11"	*Specialty Woods*	57,270.
180	5' 11"	*With Inlays, add'l*	8,626.
180	5' 11"	*With Classic Styling*	5,406.
190	6' 3"	Polished Ebony	50,026.
190	6' 3"	Polished Mahogany	52,326.
190	6' 3"	*Specialty Woods*	60,490.
190	6' 3"	*With Inlays, add'l*	9,890.
190	6' 3"	*With Classic Styling, add'l*	6,878.
M/P 192	6' 4"	*"Academy" Ebony*	81,766.
M/P 192	6' 4"	Polished Ebony	94,288.
M/P 192	6' 4"	Polished Mahogany	98,888.
M/P 192	6' 4"	*Walnut*	87,768.
M/P 192	6' 4"	*Polished Walnut*	91,748.
M/P 192	6' 4"	*Cherry*	87,768.
M/P 192	6' 4"	*Polished Cherry*	91,748.
M/P 192	6' 4"	*Polished White*	91,748.
M/P 192	6' 4"	*Specialty Woods*	107,640.
M/P 192	6' 4"	*With Inlays, add'l*	11,956.
M/P 192	6' 4"	*With Classic Styling, add'l*	8,362.
208	6' 10"	Polished Ebony (Jan. 2004)	66,010.
208	6' 10"	Polished Mahogany (Jan. 2004)	68,310.
B-210	6' 11"	*"Academy" Ebony*	95,680.
B-210	6' 11"	Polished Ebony	111,090.
B-210	6' 11"	*With Classic Styling, add'l*	9,750.
C-232	7' 6"	Polished Ebony	112,632.
D-280	9' 2"	Polished Ebony	152,582.

*For explanation of terms and prices, please see pages 42–48.

Model	Size	Style and Finish	Price*

Becker, J.

Verticals

A-121	47"	"Aurora" Polished Ebony	2,590.
A-121	47"	"Aurora" Polished Mahogany	2,590.
A-121	47"	"Aurora" Polished Oak	2,590.
A-121	47"	"Aurora" Polished Walnut	2,590.
A-122	47"	"Aurora" Chippendale Polished Ebony	2,690.
A-122	47"	"Aurora" Chippendale Pol. Mahagony	2,690.
A-122	47"	"Aurora" Chippendale Polished Oak	2,690.
A-122	47"	"Aurora" Chippendale Polished Walnut	2,690.
A-122	47"	"Aurora" Chippendale Polished White	2,890.

Grands

GP-155M	5' 2"	"Mignon" Polished Ebony	6,380.

Behning

Verticals

BE-109	43"	Continental Polished Ebony	2,790.
BE-109	43"	Continental Polished Mahogany	2,910.
BE-112D	43"	Mediterranean Oak	3,330.
BE-112D	43"	French Provincial Cherry	3,430.
BE-112D	43"	Queen Anne Oak	3,430.
BE-112T	43"	Continental Polished Ebony	2,910.
BE-112T	43"	Continental Polished Mahogany	2,990.
BE-116	46"	Institutional Ebony	3,590.
BE-116	46"	Institutional American Oak	3,790.
BE-116	46"	Institutional American Walnut	3,790.
BE-119D	47"	Mediterranean Oak	3,970.
BE-119D	47"	French Provincial Cherry	4,070.
BE-119D	47"	Queen Anne Oak	4,070.

Grands

BE-142	4' 7"	Polished Ebony	7,750.
BE-142	4' 7"	Polished Mahogany	7,950.
BE-142	4' 7"	Polished White	7,950.
BE-152	5'	Polished Ebony	8,410.
BE-152	5'	Polished Mahogany	8,610.

Model	Size	Style and Finish	Price*
BE-152	5'	Polished White	8,610.
BE-152L	5'	Louis XIV Polished Ebony	9,690.
BE-152Q	5'	Queen Anne Polished Mahogany	9,690.
BE-162	5' 4"	Polished Ebony	9,510.
BE-162	5' 4"	Polished Mahogany	9,710.
BE-162	5' 4"	Polished White	9,710.
BE-172	5' 8"	Polished Ebony	10,190.
BE-172L	5' 8"	Louis XIV Polished Ebony	11,190.
BE-172L	5' 8"	Louis XIV Polished Mahogany	11,590.
BE-172L	5' 8"	Louis XIV Polished White	11,590.
BE-182	6'	Polished Ebony	11,790.

Bergmann

Verticals

Model	Size	Style and Finish	Price*
BE-109	43"	Continental Polished Ebony	2,840.
BE-109	43"	Continental Polished Red Mahogany	2,930.
BE-109	43"	Continental Polished Brown Mahogany	2,930.
BE-109	43"	Continental Polished Ivory	2,840.
BAF-108	43"	Mahogany	3,350.
BAF-108	43"	Queen Anne Oak	3,350.
BAF-108	43"	Mediterranean Oak	3,350.
BAF-108	43"	Queen Anne Cherry	3,350.
BAF-108	43"	French Provincial Cherry	3,350.
BE-118	47"	Polished Ebony	3,350.
BE-118	47"	Polished Red Mahogany	3,470.
BAF-118	47"	Cherry	3,580.
BE-121	48"	Polished Ebony	3,560.
BE-121	48"	Polished Red Mahogany	3,680.
BE-131	52"	Polished Ebony	3,770.
BE-131	52"	Polished Red Mahogany	3,890.

Grands

Model	Size	Style and Finish	Price*
BTG-150	4' 11"	Polished Ebony	8,810.
BTG-150	4' 11"	Polished Red Mahogany	8,810.
BTG-150	4' 11"	Polished Ivory	8,810.
BTG-157	5' 2"	Polished Ebony	9,860.
BTG-157	5' 2"	Polished Red Mahogany	9,860.

*For explanation of terms and prices, please see pages 42–48.

Model	Size	Style and Finish	Price*

Bergmann (continued)

Model	Size	Style and Finish	Price*
BTG-157	5' 2"	Polished Ivory	9,860.
BTG-175	5' 9"	Polished Ebony	11,120.
BTG-185	6' 1"	Polished Ebony	11,960.

Blüthner

Prices do not include bench.

Verticals

I	45"	Ebony or Polished Ebony	20,632.
I	45"	Walnut or Polished Walnut	21,558.
I	45"	Mahogany or Polished Mahogany	21,446.
I	45"	Cherry or Polished Cherry	21,446.
I	45"	White or Polished White	21,558.
C	46"	Ebony or Polished Ebony	20,772.
C	46"	Walnut or Polished Walnut	21,812.
C	46"	Mahogany or Polished Mahogany	21,602.
C	46"	Cherry or Polished Cherry	21,706.
C	46"	White or Polished White	21,812.
C	46"	Polished Bubinga, Yew, Macassar Eby.	22,850.
C	46"	Saxony Polished Pyramid Mahogany	27,598.
C	46"	Saxony Polished Burl Walnut Inlay	27,864.
A	49"	Ebony or Polished Ebony	26,458.
A	49"	Walnut or Polished Walnut	27,780.
A	49"	Mahogany or Polished Mahogany	27,514.
A	49"	Cherry or Polished Cherry	27,648.
A	49"	White or Polished White	27,780.
A	49"	Polished Bubinga, Yew, Macassar Eby.	29,102.
A	49"	Saxony Polished Pyramid Mahogany	35,150.
A	49"	Saxony Polished Burl Walnut Inlay	35,490.
B	52"	Ebony or Polished Ebony	30,208.
B	52"	Walnut or Polished Walnut	31,718.
B	52"	Mahogany or Polished Mahogany	31,414.
B	52"	Cherry or Polished Cherry	31,564.
B	52"	White or Polished White	31,718.
B	52"	Polished Bubinga, Yew, Macassar Eby.	33,228.

Model	Size	Style and Finish	Price*
B	52"	Saxony Polished Pyramid Mahogany	40,132.
B	52"	Saxony Polished Burl Walnut Inlay	40,520.
Grands			
11	5' 1"	Ebony or Polished Ebony	53,568.
11	5' 1"	Walnut or Polished Walnut	56,246.
11	5' 1"	Mahogany or Polished Mahogany	55,648.
11	5' 1"	Cherry or Polished Cherry	55,980.
11	5' 1"	White or Polished White	56,246.
11	5' 1"	Polished Bubinga, Yew, Macassar Eby.	58,924.
11	5' 1"	Saxony Polished Pyramid Mahogany	71,172.
11	5' 1"	Saxony Polished Burl Walnut Inlay	71,856.
11	5' 1"	"President" Polished Ebony	60,222.
11	5' 1"	"President" Polished Mahogany	62,630.
11	5' 1"	"President" Polished Walnut	63,234.
11	5' 1"	"President" Polished Bubinga	66,244.
11	5' 1"	Louis XV Ebony or Polished Ebony	62,960.
11	5' 1"	Louis XV Mahogany or Pol. Mahogany	61,528.
11	5' 1"	Louis XV Walnut or Polished Walnut	66,106.
11	5' 1"	"Kaiser Wilhelm II" Polished Ebony	63,506.
11	5' 1"	"Kaiser Wilhelm II" Pol. Mahogany	66,046.
11	5' 1"	"Kaiser Wilhelm II" Polished Walnut	66,682.
11	5' 1"	"Kaiser Wilhelm II" Polished Cherry	66,366.
11	5' 1"	"Ambassador" East Indian Rosewood	73,908.
11	5' 1"	"Ambassador" Walnut	68,434.
11	5' 1"	"Nicolas II" Walnut with Burl Inlay	73,908.
11	5' 1"	Louis XVI Rococo White with Gold	79,384.
11	5' 1"	"Classic Alexandra" Polished Ebony	61,318.
11	5' 1"	"Classic Alexandra" Pol. Mahogany	63,770.
11	5' 1"	"Classic Alexandra" Polished Walnut	64,384.
10	5' 5"	Ebony or Polished Ebony	61,752.
10	5' 5"	Walnut or Polished Walnut	64,838.
10	5' 5"	Mahogany or Polished Mahogany	64,222.
10	5' 5"	Cherry or Polished Cherry	64,532.
10	5' 5"	White or Polished White	64,838.
10	5' 5"	Polished Bubinga, Yew, Macassar Eby.	67,928.
10	5' 5"	Saxony Polished Pyramid Mahogany	82,044.
10	5' 5"	Saxony Polished Burl Walnut Inlay	82,834.

*For explanation of terms and prices, please see pages 42–48.

Model	Size	Style and Finish	Price*
		Blüthner (continued)	
10	5' 5"	"President" Polished Ebony	69,424.
10	5' 5"	"President" Polished Mahogany	72,200.
10	5' 5"	"President" Polished Walnut	72,894.
10	5' 5"	"President" Polished Bubinga	76,364.
10	5' 5"	"Senator" French Walnut with Leather	75,734.
10	5' 5"	"Senator" Jacaranda Rosewd w/Leather	80,782.
10	5' 5"	Louis XV Ebony or Polished Ebony	72,578.
10	5' 5"	Louis XV Mahogany or Pol. Mahogany	69,058.
10	5' 5"	Louis XV Walnut or Polished Walnut	76,208.
10	5' 5"	"Kaiser Wilhelm II" Polished Ebony	73,210.
10	5' 5"	"Kaiser Wilhelm II" Pol. Mahogany	76,138.
10	5' 5"	"Kaiser Wilhelm II" Polished Walnut	76,870.
10	5' 5"	"Kaiser Wilhelm II" Polished Cherry	76,502.
10	5' 5"	"Ambassador" East Indian Rosewood	85,200.
10	5' 5"	"Ambassador" Walnut	78,890.
10	5' 5"	"Nicolas II" Walnut with Burl Inlay	85,200.
10	5' 5"	Louis XVI Rococo White with Gold	91,512.
10	5' 5"	"Classic Alexandra" Polished Ebony	70,684.
10	5' 5"	"Classic Alexandra" Pol. Mahogany	73,512.
10	5' 5"	"Classic Alexandra" Polished Walnut	74,220.
6	6' 3"	Ebony or Polished Ebony	67,350.
6	6' 3"	Walnut or Polished Walnut	70,718.
6	6' 3"	Mahogany or Polished Mahogany	70,044.
6	6' 3"	Cherry or Polished Cherry	70,384.
6	6' 3"	White or Polished White	70,718.
6	6' 3"	Polished Bubinga, Yew, Macassar Eby.	74,086.
6	6' 3"	Saxony Polished Pyramid Mahogany	89,484.
6	6' 3"	Saxony Polished Burl Walnut Inlay	90,346.
6	6' 3"	"President" Polished Ebony	75,718.
6	6' 3"	"President" Polished Mahogany	78,746.
6	6' 3"	"President" Polished Walnut	79,506.
6	6' 3"	"President" Polished Bubinga	83,290.
6	6' 3"	"Senator" French Walnut with Leather	82,602.
6	6' 3"	"Senator" Jacaranda Rosewd w/Leather	88,108.
6	6' 3"	Louis XV Ebony or Polished Ebony	79,160.

Model	Size	Style and Finish	Price*
6	6' 3"	Louis XV Mahogany or Pol. Mahogany	83,116.
6	6' 3"	Louis XV Walnut or Polished Walnut	77,872.
6	6' 3"	"Kaiser Wilhelm II" Polished Ebony	79,848.
6	6' 3"	"Kaiser Wilhelm II" Pol. Mahogany	83,044.
6	6' 3"	"Kaiser Wilhelm II" Polished Walnut	83,840.
6	6' 3"	"Kaiser Wilhelm II" Polished Cherry	83,440.
6	6' 3"	"Ambassador" East Indian Rosewood	92,926.
6	6' 3"	"Ambassador" Walnut	86,044.
6	6' 3"	"Nicolas II" Walnut with Burl Inlay	92,926.
6	6' 3"	Louis XVI Rococo White with Gold	99,810.
6	6' 3"	"Classic Alexandra" Polished Ebony	77,094.
6	6' 3"	"Classic Alexandra" Pol. Mahogany	80,950.
6	6' 3"	"Classic Alexandra" Polished Walnut	80,178.
4	6' 10"	Ebony or Polished Ebony	79,882.
4	6' 10"	Walnut or Polished Walnut	83,876.
4	6' 10"	Mahogany or Polished Mahogany	83,076.
4	6' 10"	Cherry or Polished Cherry	83,478.
4	6' 10"	White or Polished White	83,876.
4	6' 10"	Polished Bubinga, Yew, Macassar Eby.	87,870.
4	6' 10"	Saxony Polished Pyramid Mahogany	106,134.
4	6' 10"	Saxony Polished Burl Walnut Inlay	107,154.
4	6' 10"	"President" Polished Ebony	89,804.
4	6' 10"	"President" Polished Mahogany	93,398.
4	6' 10"	"President" Polished Walnut	94,296.
4	6' 10"	"President" Polished Bubinga	98,786.
4	6' 10"	"Kaiser Wilhelm II" Polished Ebony	94,704.
4	6' 10"	"Kaiser Wilhelm II" Pol. Mahogany	98,490.
4	6' 10"	"Kaiser Wilhelm II" Polished Walnut	99,438.
4	6' 10"	"Kaiser Wilhelm II" Polished Cherry	98,964.
4	6' 10"	"Ambassador" East Indian Rosewood	110,216.
4	6' 10"	"Ambassador" Walnut	102,052.
4	6' 10"	"Classic Alexandra" Polished Ebony	91,438.
4	6' 10"	"Classic Alexandra" Pol. Mahogany	96,010.
4	6' 10"	"Classic Alexandra" Polished Walnut	95,094.
2	7' 8"	Ebony or Polished Ebony	89,280.
2	7' 8"	Walnut or Polished Walnut	93,744.
2	7' 8"	Mahogany or Polished Mahogany	92,850.

*For explanation of terms and prices, please see pages 42–48.

Blüthner (continued)

Model	Size	Style and Finish	Price*
2	7' 8"	Cherry or Polished Cherry	93,298.
2	7' 8"	White or Polished White	93,744.
2	7' 8"	Polished Bubinga, Yew, Macassar Eby.	98,208.
2	7' 8"	Saxony Polished Pyramid Mahogany	118,620.
2	7' 8"	Saxony Polished Burl Walnut Inlay	119,760.
2	7' 8"	"President" Polished Ebony	100,370.
2	7' 8"	"President" Polished Mahogany	104,384.
2	7' 8"	"President" Polished Walnut	105,390.
2	7' 8"	"President" Polished Bubinga	110,408.
2	7' 8"	"Kaiser Wilhelm II" Polished Ebony	105,844.
2	7' 8"	"Kaiser Wilhelm II" Pol. Mahogany	110,078.
2	7' 8"	"Kaiser Wilhelm II" Polished Walnut	111,138.
2	7' 8"	"Kaiser Wilhelm II" Polished Cherry	110,608.
2	7' 8"	"Ambassador" East Indian Rosewood	123,182.
2	7' 8"	"Ambassador" Walnut	114,058.
1	9' 2"	Ebony or Polished Ebony	106,508.
1	9' 2"	Walnut or Polished Walnut	111,834.
1	9' 2"	Mahogany or Polished Mahogany	110,768.
1	9' 2"	Cherry or Polished Cherry	111,302.
1	9' 2"	White or Polished White	111,834.
1	9' 2"	"President" Polished Ebony	119,740.
1	9' 2"	"President" Polished Mahogany	124,530.
1	9' 2"	"President" Polished Walnut	125,726.
1	9' 2"	"President" Polished Bubinga	131,714.
—	—	*Jubilee Edition Plate, any model, add'l*	5,980.

Bohemia

Verticals

Model	Size	Style and Finish	Price*
118	47"	Continental Polished Ebony	5,940.
118	47"	Continental Open-pore Walnut	5,700.
118	47"	Continental Polished Walnut	6,100.
118	47"	Continental Open-pore Mahogany	5,700.
118	47"	Continental Polished Mahogany	6,100.
118	47"	Continental Open-pore Oak	5,700.

Model	Size	Style and Finish	Price*
118	47"	Continental Open-pore Cherry	5,940.
118	47"	Continental Polished White	6,160.
122	48"	Demi-Chippendale Polished Ebony	6,280.
122	48"	Demi-Chippendale Polished Walnut	6,460.
122	48"	Demi-Chippendale Polished Mahogany	6,460.
122	48"	*Demi-Chippendale Pomele*	6,760.
122	48"	Chippendale Polished Ebony	6,900.
122	48"	Chippendale Polished Walnut	7,100.
122	48"	Chippendale Polished Mahogany	7,100.
122	48"	*"Romance" with Mahogany Oval*	7,260.
123	48"	Polished Ebony	6,220.
123	48"	Open-pore Walnut	5,960.
123	48"	Polished Walnut	6,380.
123	48"	Open-pore Mahogany	5,960.
123	48"	Polished Mahogany	6,380.
123	48"	Open-pore Oak	5,960.
123	48"	Open-pore Cherry	6,220.
123	48"	Polished White	6,500.
123	48"	*Pomele*	6,580.
123	48"	*with Mahogany Oval*	6,580.
125	49"	Polished Ebony	6,760.
125	49"	Polished Walnut	6,960.
125	49"	Polished Mahogany	6,960.
125	49"	Open-pore Cherry	6,760.
125	49"	Polished White	7,040.
125	49"	*Pomele*	7,260.
125BR	49"	Polished Ebony	7,860.
125BR	49"	Polished Walnut	8,100.
125BR	49"	Polished Mahogany	8,100.
125BR	49"	Open-pore Cherry	7,860.
132	53"	Polished Ebony	7,660.
132BR	53"	Polished Ebony	8,900.
Grands			
156A-D	5' 1"	Ebony and Polished Ebony	21,520.
156A-D	5' 1"	Walnut and Polished Walnut	23,760.
156A-D	5' 1"	Mahogany and Polished Mahogany	23,760.
156A-D	5' 1"	Polished White	22,640.

*For explanation of terms and prices, please see pages 42–48.

Model	Size	Style and Finish	Price*

Bohemia (continued)

Model	Size	Style and Finish	Price*
156BR	5' 1"	Ebony and Polished Ebony	22,080.
156BR	5' 1"	Walnut and Polished Walnut	24,320.
156BR	5' 1"	Mahogany and Polished Mahogany	24,320.
156BR	5' 1"	Polished White	23,200.
156BR	5' 1"	*Demi-Chip. Walnut and Pol. Walnut*	25,800.
156BR	5' 1"	*Demi-Chip. Mahogany and Pol. Mahog.*	25,800.
156BR	5' 1"	*Chippendale Walnut and Pol. Walnut*	26,540.
156BR	5' 1"	*Chippendale Mahog. and Pol. Mahog.*	26,540.
156D	5' 1"	*Demi-Chip. Walnut and Pol. Walnut*	25,240.
156D	5' 1"	*Demi-Chip. Mahog. and Pol. Mahog.*	25,240.
156D	5' 1"	*Chippendale Walnut and Pol. Walnut*	25,980.
156D	5' 1"	*Chippendale Mahog. and Pol. Mahog.*	25,980.
185A-BR	6' 1"	*Empire Polished Ebony*	27,140.
185A-D	6' 1"	Ebony and Polished Ebony	25,180.
185A-D	6' 1"	Walnut and Polished Walnut	27,780.
185A-D	6' 1"	Mahogany and Polished Mahogany	27,780.
185A-D	6' 1"	Polished White	26,480.
185A-D	6' 1"	*Empire Polished Ebony*	26,580.
185BR	6' 1"	Ebony and Polished Ebony	25,740.
185BR	6' 1"	Walnut and Polished Walnut	28,340.
185BR	6' 1"	Mahogany and Polished Mahogany	28,340.
185BR	6' 1"	Polished White	27,040.

Bösendorfer

Verticals

Model	Size	Style and Finish	Price*
130	52"	175th Anniversary, Polished Ebony	38,880.
130CL	52"	Polished Ebony	38,880.
130CL	52"	Polished, Satin, Open-pore: Walnut, Mahogany, Pomele, Cherry, Bubinga, Wenga, White	40,880.
130CL	52"	Polished, Satin, Open-pore: Pyramid Mahogany, Amboyna, Rio Rosewood, Burl Walnut, Birdseye Maple, Yew, Macassar	42,880.

Model	Size	Style and Finish	Price*
Grands			
170	5' 8"	Polished Ebony	76,980.
170	5' 8"	Polished, Satin, Open-pore: Walnut, Mahogany, Pomele, Cherry, Bubinga, Wenga, White	81,600.
170	5' 8"	Polished, Satin, Open-pore: Pyramid Mahogany, Amboyna, Rio Rosewood, Burl Walnut, Birdseye Maple, Yew, Macassar	86,600.
170	5' 8"	"Johann Strauss" Polished Ebony	81,600.
170	5' 8"	"Johann Strauss" Polished, any finish	90,120.
170	5' 8"	"Franz Schubert" Polished Ebony	81,600.
170	5' 8"	"Franz Schubert" Polished, any finish	90,120.
170	5' 8"	"Vienna," any finish	90,120.
170	5' 8"	"Senator," any finish	85,720.
170	5' 8"	"Chopin," any finish	106,320.
170	5' 8"	"Classic" Rio Rosewood	87,920.
170	5' 8"	"Yacht," any finish	87,920.
170	5' 8"	Chippendale, any finish	80,980.
170	5' 8"	Louis XV, any finish	96,980.
170	5' 8"	Baroque, any finish	96,980.
175	5' 8"	175th Anniversary, Polished Ebony	55,320.
185CS	6' 1"	"Conservatory" Ebony	57,520.
185	6' 1"	Polished Ebony	80,400.
185	6' 1"	Polished, Satin, Open-pore: Walnut, Mahogany, Pomele, Cherry, Bubinga, Wenga, White	87,000.
185	6' 1"	Polished, Satin, Open-pore: Pyramid Mahogany, Amboyna, Rio Rosewood, Burl Walnut, Birdseye Maple, Yew, Macassar	92,400.
185	6' 1"	"Johann Strauss" Polished Ebony	87,000.
185	6' 1"	"Johann Strauss" Polished, any finish	94,120.
185	6' 1"	"Franz Schubert" Polished Ebony	87,000.
185	6' 1"	"Franz Schubert" Polished, any finish	94,120.
185	6' 1"	"Vienna," any finish	94,120.

*For explanation of terms and prices, please see pages 42–48.

Model	Size	Style and Finish	Price*
Bösendorfer (continued)			
185	6' 1"	"Senator," any finish	89,720.
185	6' 1"	"Chopin," any finish	110,320.
185	6' 1"	"Classic" Rio Rosewood	91,920.
185	6' 1"	"Yacht," any finish	91,920.
185	6' 1"	"Porsche Design," any color	110,320.
185	6' 1"	Chippendale, any finish	84,400.
185	6' 1"	Louis XV, any finish	100,400.
185	6' 1"	Baroque, any finish	100,400.
200CS	6' 7"	"Conservatory" Ebony	59,600.
200	6' 7"	Polished Ebony	88,720.
200	6' 7"	Polished, Satin, Open-pore: Walnut, Mahogany, Pomele, Cherry, Bubinga, Wenga, White	96,600.
200	6' 7"	Polished, Satin, Open-pore: Pyramid Mahogany, Amboyna, Rio Rosewood, Burl Walnut, Birdseye Maple, Yew, Macassar	101,200.
200	6' 7"	"Johann Strauss" Polished Ebony	96,600.
200	6' 7"	"Johann Strauss" Polished, any finish	102,120.
200	6' 7"	"Franz Schubert" Polished Ebony	96,600.
200	6' 7"	"Franz Schubert" Polished, any finish	102,120.
200	6' 7"	"Vienna," any finish	102,120.
200	6' 7"	"Senator," any finish	97,760.
200	6' 7"	"Chopin," any finish	118,320.
200	6' 7"	"Classic" Rio Rosewood	99,400.
200	6' 7"	"Yacht," any finish	99,400.
200	6' 7"	Chippendale, any finish	92,720.
200	6' 7"	Louis XV, any finish	108,720.
200	6' 7"	Baroque, any finish	108,720.
214CS	7'	"Conservatory" Ebony	65,800.
214	7'	Polished Ebony	103,320.
214	7'	Polished, Satin, Open-pore: Walnut, Mahogany, Pomele, Cherry, Bubinga, Wenga, White	109,800.

Model	Size	Style and Finish	Price*
214	7'	Polished, Satin, Open-pore: Pyramid Mahogany, Amboyna, Rio Rosewood, Burl Walnut, Birdseye Maple, Yew, Macassar	113,600.
214	7'	"Johann Strauss" Polished Ebony	109,800.
214	7'	"Johann Strauss" Polished, any finish	116,120.
214	7'	"Franz Schubert" Polished Ebony	109,800.
214	7'	"Franz Schubert" Polished, any finish	116,120.
214	7'	"Vienna," any finish	116,120.
214	7'	"Senator," any finish	111,720.
214	7'	"Chopin," any finish	132,320.
214	7'	"Classic" Rio Rosewood	111,200.
214	7'	"Yacht," any finish	111,200.
214	7'	"Porsche Design," any color	132,320.
214	7'	Chippendale, any finish	107,320.
214	7'	Louis XV, any finish	123,320.
214	7'	Baroque, any finish	123,320.
225	7' 4"	Polished Ebony	109,320.
225	7' 4"	Polished, Satin, Open-pore: Walnut, Mahogany, Pomele, Cherry, Bubinga, Wenga, White	119,000.
225	7' 4"	Polished, Satin, Open-pore: Pyramid Mahogany, Amboyna, Rio Rosewood, Burl Walnut, Birdseye Maple, Yew, Macassar	124,000.
225	7' 4"	"Johann Strauss" Polished Ebony	119,000.
225	7' 4"	"Johann Strauss" Polished, any finish	120,120.
225	7' 4"	"Franz Schubert" Polished Ebony	119,000.
225	7' 4"	"Franz Schubert" Polished, any finish	120,120.
225	7' 4"	"Vienna," any finish	120,120.
225	7' 4"	"Senator," any finish	115,720.
225	7' 4"	"Chopin," any finish	132,320.
225	7' 4"	"Classic" Rio Rosewood	114,600.
225	7' 4"	"Yacht," any finish	114,600.
225	7' 4"	Chippendale, any finish	113,320.
225	7' 4"	Louis XV, any finish	129,320.

*For explanation of terms and prices, please see pages 42–48.

Model	Size	Style and Finish	Price*

Bösendorfer (continued)

Model	Size	Style and Finish	Price*
225	7' 4"	Baroque, any finish	129,320.
280	9' 2"	Polished Ebony	142,000.
280	9' 2"	Polished, Satin, Open-pore: Walnut, Mahogany, Pomele, Cherry, Bubinga, Wenga, White	152,000.
280	9' 2"	Polished, Satin, Open-pore: Pyramid Mahogany, Amboyna, Rio Rosewood, Burl Walnut, Birdseye Maple, Yew, Macassar	158,000.
280	9' 2"	"Johann Strauss" Polished Ebony	152,000.
280	9' 2"	"Johann Strauss" Polished, any finish	158,120.
280	9' 2"	"Franz Schubert" Polished Ebony	152,000.
280	9' 2"	"Franz Schubert" Polished, any finish	158,120.
280	9' 2"	"Vienna," any finish	158,120.
280	9' 2"	"Senator," any finish	153,720.
280	9' 2"	"Chopin," any finish	174,320.
280	9' 2"	"Classic" Rio Rosewood	153,000.
280	9' 2"	"Yacht," any finish	153,000.
280	9' 2"	"Porsche Design," any color	174,320.
280	9' 2"	Chippendale, any finish	147,000.
280	9' 2"	Louis XV, any finish	166,000.
280	9' 2"	Baroque, any finish	166,000.
290	9' 6"	Polished Ebony	162,000.
290	9' 6"	Polished, Satin, Open-pore: Walnut, Mahogany, Pomele, Cherry, Bubinga, Wenga, White	172,000.
290	9' 6"	Polished, Satin, Open-pore: Pyramid Mahogany, Amboyna, Rio Rosewood, Burl Walnut, Birdseye Maple, Yew, Macassar	178,000.
290	9' 6"	"Johann Strauss" Polished Ebony	172,000.
290	9' 6"	"Johann Strauss" Polished, any finish	178,120.
290	9' 6"	"Franz Schubert" Polished Ebony	172,000.
290	9' 6"	"Franz Schubert" Polished, any finish	178,120.
290	9' 6"	"Vienna," any finish	178,120.

Model	Size	Style and Finish	Price*
290	9' 6"	"Senator," any finish	173,720.
290	9' 6"	"Chopin," any finish	196,320.
290	9' 6"	"Classic" Rio Rosewood	172,400.
290	9' 6"	"Yacht," any finish	172,400.
290	9' 6"	Chippendale, any finish	167,000.
290	9' 6"	Louis XV, any finish	186,000.
290	9' 6"	Baroque, any finish	186,000.

Boston

Verticals

UP-118C	45"	Continental Polished Ebony	7,960.
UP-118C	45"	Continental Polished Walnut	8,680.
UP-118C	45"	Continental Polished Mahogany	8,680.
UP-118E II	46"	Polished Ebony	8,990.
UP-118E II	46"	Walnut	10,040.
UP-118E II	46"	Polished Walnut	10,250.
UP-118E II	46"	Polished Mahogany	10,250.
UP-118E II	46"	Polished White	10,040.
UP-118A	46"	Art Deco Aniegre	7,990.
UP-118T	46"	Florentine Mahogany	7,990.
UP-118P	46"	Berkshire Cherry	7,990.
UP-118S	46"	Open-Pore Honey Oak	5,990.
UP-118S	46"	Open-Pore Black Oak	5,990.
UP-118S	46"	Open-Pore Red Oak	5,990.
UP-118S	46"	Mahogany	7,400.
UP-126E	50"	Polished Ebony	10,900.
UP-126E	50"	Polished Mahogany	12,580.
UP-132E II	52"	Polished Ebony	11,980.

Grands

GP-156	5' 1"	Ebony and Polished Ebony	15,720.
GP-163	5' 4"	Ebony	18,880.
GP-163	5' 4"	Polished Ebony	19,300.
GP-163	5' 4"	Mahogany	20,560.
GP-163	5' 4"	Polished Mahogany	21,040.
GP-163	5' 4"	Walnut	20,760.
GP-163	5' 4"	Polished Walnut	21,280.

*For explanation of terms and prices, please see pages 42–48.

Model	Size	Style and Finish	Price*

Boston (continued)

Model	Size	Style and Finish	Price*
GP-163	5' 4"	Polished White	19,840.
GP-163	5' 4"	Polished Ivory	19,840.
GP-178	5' 10"	Ebony	21,780.
GP-178	5' 10"	Polished Ebony	22,240.
GP-178	5' 10"	Mahogany	23,200.
GP-178	5' 10"	Polished Mahogany	23,700.
GP-178	5' 10"	Walnut	23,460.
GP-178	5' 10"	Polished Walnut	24,160.
GP-178	5' 10"	Polished White	22,720.
GP-178	5' 10"	Polished Ivory	22,720.
GP-193	6' 4"	Ebony	27,580.
GP-193	6' 4"	Polished Ebony	28,280.
GP-193	6' 4"	Walnut	30,720.
GP-193	6' 4"	Polished Mahogany	30,940.
GP-193	6' 4"	Polished White	29,760.
GP-218	7' 2"	Ebony	35,020.
GP-218	7' 2"	Polished Ebony	35,920.

Breitmann

Verticals

Model	Size	Style and Finish	Price*
B110	43-1/4"	Polished Ebony	3,060.
B110	43-1/4"	Polished Mahogany	3,120.
B110	43-1/4"	Polished Walnut	3,120.
B120	48"	Polished Ebony	3,502.
B120	48"	Polished Mahogany	3,640.
B120	48"	Polished Walnut	3,640.
B122	49"	Polished Ebony	3,924.
B122	49"	Polished Mahogany	4,126.
B122	49"	Polished Walnut	4,126.
B130	52"	Polished Ebony	4,220.
B130	52"	Polished Mahogany	4,560.
B130	52"	Polished Walnut	4,560.
B130	52"	Polished White	4,320.

Grands

Model	Size	Style and Finish	Price*
B116	5' 3"	Polished Ebony	8,906.
B116	5' 3"	Polished White	9,040.

Cable, Hobart M.

Verticals

Model	Size	Style and Finish	Price*
UH 09	42-1/2"	Continental Polished Ebony	2,790.
UH 09	42-1/2"	Continental Polished Mahogany	2,910.
UH 09	42-1/2"	Continental Polished Walnut	2,910.
UH 09	42-1/2"	Continental Cherry	2,830.
UH 09	42-1/2"	Continental Polished White	2,910.
UH 09L	42-1/2"	Continental (w/toe) Polished Ebony	2,870.
UH 09L	42-1/2"	Continental (w/toe) Polished Mahogany	2,990.
UH 09L	42-1/2"	Continental (w/toe) Polished Walnut	2,990.
UH 09L	42-1/2"	Continental (w/toe) Cherry	2,910.
UH 09L	42-1/2"	Continental (w/toe) Polished White	2,990.
CH 12F	44"	French Provincial Cherry	3,270.
CH 12F	44"	French Provincial Oak	3,270.
CH 12M	44"	Mediterranean Oak	3,270.
UH 12TT	44"	Polished Ebony	2,990.
UH 12TT	44"	Polished Mahogany	3,110.
UH 12TT	44"	Polished Walnut	3,110.
UH 12TT	44"	Cherry	3,030.
UH 12TT	44"	Polished White	3,110.
CH 19F	47"	French Provincial Cherry	3,590.
CH 19F	47"	French Provincial Oak	3,590.
CH 19M	47"	Mediterranean Oak	3,590.
UH 19ST	47"	Polished Ebony	3,110.
UH 19ST	47"	Polished Mahogany	3,230.
UH 19ST	47"	Polished Walnut	3,230.
UH 19ST	47"	Oak	3,140.
UH 19ST	47"	Polished White	3,230.
UH 19F	47"	French Polished Ebony	3,230.
UH 19F	47"	French Polished Mahogany	3,350.
UH 19F	47"	French Polished Walnut	3,350.
UH 19F	47"	French Polished White	3,350.
UH 22T	49"	Polished Ebony	3,320.
UH 22T	49"	Polished Mahogany	3,380.
UH 22T	49"	Polished Walnut	3,380.
UH 22T	49"	Polished White	3,380.

*For explanation of terms and prices, please see pages 42–48.

Model	Size	Style and Finish	Price*

Cable, Hobart M. (continued)

Model	Size	Style and Finish	Price*
UH 22F	49"	French Polished Ebony	3,380.
UH 22F	49"	French Polished Mahogany	3,440.
UH 22F	49"	French Polished Walnut	3,440.
UH 32T	52"	Polished Ebony	3,480.
UH 32T	52"	Polished Mahogany	3,540.
UH 32T	52"	Polished Walnut	3,540.
Grands			
GH 42	4' 8"	Polished Ebony	8,200.
GH 42	4' 8"	Polished Mahogany	8,300.
GH 42	4' 8"	Polished Walnut	8,300.
GH 42	4' 8"	Polished White	8,300.
GH 42F	4' 8"	French Polished Mahogany	8,700.
GH 42F	4' 8"	French Polished Walnut	8,700.
GH 52	5'	Polished Ebony	8,960.
GH 52	5'	Polished Mahogany	9,160.
GH 52	5'	Polished Walnut	9,160.
GH 52	5'	Polished White	9,060.
GH 62	5' 4"	Polished Ebony	9,920.
GH 62	5' 4"	Polished Mahogany	10,120.
GH 62	5' 4"	Polished Walnut	10,120.
GH 62	5' 4"	Polished Oak	10,020.
GH 62	5' 4"	Polished White	10,020.
GH 62F	5' 4"	French Provincial Polished Mahogany	10,220.
GH 62F	5' 4"	French Provincial Polished Walnut	10,420.
GH 62F	5' 4"	French Provincial Polished White	10,320.
GH 72	5' 8"	Polished Ebony	10,600.
GH 72	5' 8"	Polished Mahogany	10,800.
GH 72	5' 8"	Polished Walnut	10,800.
GH 72	5' 8"	Polished Oak	11,000.
GH 72	5' 8"	Polished White	11,000.
GH 87	6' 2"	Polished Ebony	11,990.
GH 87	6' 2"	Polished Mahogany	12,190.
GH 87	6' 2"	Polished Walnut	12,190.

Charles R. Walter — see "Walter, Charles R."

Chase, A. B.

Verticals

Model	Size	Style and Finish	Price*
AB-112	44"	Continental Polished Ebony	2,590.
AB-112	44"	Continental Polished Mahogany	2,700.
AB-113	45"	Polished Ebony	2,790.
AB-113	45"	Polished Mahogany	2,900.
AB-121	48"	Polished Ebony	3,190.
AB-121	48"	Polished Mahogany	3,300.

Grands

AB-152	5'	Polished Ebony	7,780.
AB-152	5'	Polished Mahogany	8,280.
AB-165	5' 5"	Polished Ebony	8,780.
AB-165	5' 5"	Polished Mahogany	9,280.

Chickering

Grands

Model	Size	Style and Finish	Price*
CH162	5' 4"	Ebony and Polished Ebony	14,190.
CH162	5' 4"	Polished White	14,190.
CH162FP	5' 4"	French Provincial Cherry	17,190.
CH162QA	5' 4"	Queen Anne Cherry	17,190.
CH176	5' 9"	Polished Ebony	16,390.
CH176	5' 9"	Polished Ivory	16,390.
CH176FP	5' 9"	French Provincial Cherry	19,790.
CH176CD	5' 9"	Chippendale Cherry	19,790.
CH176L	5' 9"	Louis XV Polished Mahogany	19,790.
CH189	6' 2"	Ebony and Polished Ebony	19,190.
CH189L	6' 2"	Louis XV Polished Mahogany	23,190.

Conn

Verticals

Model	Size	Style and Finish	Price*
C433	43"	French Cherry	2,790.
C434	43"	French Oak	2,790.
C435	43"	Oak	2,790.
C436	43"	Cherry	2,790.

*For explanation of terms and prices, please see pages 42–48.

Conover Cable

In general, "Wood Finishes" means mahogany, walnut, cherry, and brown oak. However, even where not specifically indicated, most models are available by special order in any finish.

Verticals

Model	Size	Style and Finish	Price
CC-142	42"	Continental Ebony	3,140.
CC-142	42"	Continental Polished Ebony	3,040.
CC-142	42"	Continental Satin/Pol. Wood Finishes	3,140.
CC-142	42"	Continental Polished Ivory/White	3,140.
CC-144F	44"	French Provincial Wood Finishes	3,840.
CC-144M	44"	Mediterranean Wood Finishes	3,740.
CC-144T	44"	Wood Finishes	3,840.
CC-112RI	45"	Ebony	3,340.
CC-112RI	45"	Polished Ebony	3,240.
CC-112RI	45"	Satin/Polished Wood Finishes	3,340.
CC-112RI	45"	Polished Ivory/White	3,340.
CC-118F	46-1/2"	French Provincial Wood Finishes	4,440.
CC-118M	46-1/2"	Mediterranean Wood Finishes	4,240.
CC-118T	46-1/2"	Wood Finishes	4,440.
CC-247	46-1/2"	Ebony and Polished Ebony	4,940.
CC-247	46-1/2"	Satin and Polished Wood Finishes	4,940.
CC-121F	48"	French Provincial Ebony	4,540.
CC-121F	48"	French Provincial Polished Ebony	4,340.
CC-121F	48"	French Prov. Satin/Pol. Wood Finishes	4,540.
CC-121M	48"	Mediterranean Ebony	4,540.
CC-121M	48"	Mediterranean Polished Ebony	4,260.
CC-121M	48"	Mediterranean Satin/Pol. Wood Finishes	4,540.

Grands

Model	Size	Style and Finish	Price
CCIG-50	4' 11-1/2"	Ebony	8,940.
CCIG-50	4' 11-1/2"	Polished Ebony	8,340.
CCIG-50	4' 11-1/2"	Polished Mahogany	8,940.
CCIG-50	4' 11-1/2"	Polished Walnut	8,940.
CCIG-50	4' 11-1/2"	Polished Ivory/White	8,940.
CCIG-54	5' 3"	Ebony	10,340.
CCIG-54	5' 3"	Polished Ebony	9,940.
CCIG-54	5' 3"	Polished Mahogany	10,340.

Model	Size	Style and Finish	Price*
CCIG-54	5' 3"	Polished Walnut	10,340.
CCIG-54	5' 3"	Polished Ivory/White	10,340.
CC-172	5' 7"	Ebony	14,140.
CC-172	5' 7"	Polished Ebony	13,540.
CC-172	5' 7"	Satin and Polished Wood Finishes	14,140.
CC-172	5' 7"	Polished Ivory/White	14,140.
CC-172L	5' 7"	Empire Ebony	15,140.
CC-172L	5' 7"	Emprie Polished Ebony	14,540.
CC-172L	5' 7"	Empire Satin/Polished Wood Finishes	15,140.
CC-172L	5' 7"	Empire Polished Ivory/White	15,140.
CC-185	6' 1"	Ebony	14,940.
CC-185	6' 1"	Polished Ebony	14,340.
CC-185	6' 1"	Satin and Polished Wood Finishes	14,940.
CC-185	6' 1"	Polished Ivory/White	14,940.
CC-185L	6' 1"	Empire Ebony	15,940.
CC-185L	6' 1"	Empire Polished Ebony	15,340.
CC-185L	6' 1"	Empire Satin and Pol. Wood Finishes	15,940.
CC-185L	6' 1"	Empire Polished Ivory/White	15,940.

Ebel, Carl / Kingsburg

Verticals

Model	Size	Style and Finish	Price*
LF-109AB	43"	Continental Polished Ebony	4,180.
LF-109AC	43"	Continental Polished Mahogany	4,270.
LF-109AC	43"	Continental Polished Walnut	4,270.
LF-109AC	43"	Continental Polished White	4,270.
LF-109AS	43"	Continental Cherry	4,270.
LF-109AS	43"	Continental Oak	4,270.
LF-109BF	43"	Continental Polished Ebony w/Molding	4,480.
LF-109AF	43"	Continental Pol. Mahogany w/Molding	4,630.
LF-109AF	43"	Continental Polished Walnut w/Molding	4,630.
LF-109BB	43"	Polished Ebony (straight leg)	4,480.
LF-109BC	43"	Polished Mahogany (straight leg)	4,480.
LF-109BC	43"	Polished Walnut (straight leg)	4,480.
LF-109BC	43"	Polished White (straight leg)	4,480.
LF-109EF	43"	Polished Ebony (curved leg)	4,630.
LF-109EF	43"	Polished Mahogany (curved leg)	4,780.

*For explanation of terms and prices, please see pages 42–48.

Model	Size	Style and Finish	Price*

Ebel, Carl / Kingsburg (continued)

Model	Size	Style and Finish	Price*
LF-109EF	43"	Polished Walnut (curved leg)	4,780.
LF-113G	44"	Queen Anne or Mediterranean Walnut	5,340.
LF-113G	44"	Queen Anne or Mediterranean Cherry	5,340.
LF-113G	44"	Queen Anne or Mediterranean Oak	5,340.
LM-115BB	45"	Polished Ebony	4,630.
LM-115BC	45"	Polished Mahogany	4,780.
LM-115BC	45"	Polished Walnut	4,780.
LM-115BF	45"	Polished Ebony with Molding	4,990.
LM-115BF	45"	Polished Mahogany with Molding	4,990.
LM-115BF	45"	Polished Walnut with Molding	4,990.
LM-115G	45"	Walnut	4,930.
LM-115G	45"	Cherry	4,930.
LM-115G	45"	Oak	4,930.
LM-116EF	46"	Chippendale Polished Ebony	4,780.
LM-116EF	46"	Chippendale Pol. Mahogany w/Molding	4,990.
LM-116EF	46"	Chippendale Pol. Walnut w/Molding	4,990.
LM-116H	46"	Polished Ebony (straight leg)	4,780.
LM-116H	46"	Polished Mahogany (straight leg)	5,090.
LM-116H	46"	Polished Walnut (straight leg)	5,090.
LM-116H	46"	Polished Oak (straight leg)	5,090.
LM-116H	46"	Polished White (straight leg)	5,090.
LM-116H	46"	Pol. Ebony w/Mahog or Walnut Accents	4,780.
LM-117CW	46"	Walnut	5,980.
LM-117GW	46"	Walnut (curved leg)	5,980.
LT-122BB	48"	Polished Ebony (straight leg)	5,530.
LT-122BC	48"	Polished Mahogany (straight leg)	5,830.
LT-122BC	48"	Polished Walnut (straight leg)	5,830.
LT-122BC	48"	Polished White (straight leg)	5,830.
LT-122BF	48"	Pol. Ebony w/Molding (straight leg)	5,980.
LT-122BF	48"	Pol. Mahogany w/Molding (straight leg)	5,980.
LT-122BF	48"	Pol. Walnut w/Molding (straight leg)	5,980.
LT-125GW	49"	Walnut	6,280.
LT-125GW	49"	Cherry	6,280.
LT-125GW	49"	Oak	6,280.

Model	Size	Style and Finish	Price*
Grands			
F-150BB	4' 11"	Polished Ebony	9,990.
F-150BC	4' 11"	Polished Mahogany	10,490.
F-150BC	4' 11"	Polished Walnut	10,490.
F-150BC	4' 11"	Polished White	10,490.
F-158BB	5' 2"	Polished Ebony	14,380.
F-158BC	5' 2"	Polished Mahogany	14,980.
F-158BC	5' 2"	Polished Walnut	14,980.
F-158BC	5' 2"	Polished Oak	14,980.
F-158BC	5' 2"	Polished White	14,980.
F-158BC	5' 2"	Polished Ivory	14,980.
F-158BS	5' 2"	Walnut	14,980.
F-158CB	5' 2"	Polished Ebony (round leg)	15,580.
F-158CC	5' 2"	Polished Mahogany (round leg)	15,580.
F-158CC	5' 2"	Polished Walnut (round leg)	15,580.
F-158E	5' 2"	Polished Ebony (French leg)	15,880.
F-158E	5' 2"	Polished Mahogany (French leg)	15,880.
F-158E	5' 2"	Polished Walnut (French leg)	15,880.
F-185BB	6' 1"	Polished Ebony	16,480.
F-185BC	6' 1"	Polished Mahogany	17,380.
F-185BC	6' 1"	Walnut	17,380.
F-185BC	6' 1"	Polished Walnut	17,380.
F-185BC	6' 1"	Polished White	17,380.
F-185BC	6' 1"	Polished Ivory	17,380.
F-185CC	6' 1"	Polished Mahogany (round leg)	17,980.
F-185CC	6' 1"	Polished Walnut (round leg)	17,980.
F-185E	6' 1"	Polished Ebony (French leg)	17,980.
F-185E	6' 1"	Polished Mahogany (French leg)	17,980.
F-185E	6' 1"	Polished Walnut (French leg)	17,980.

Ellington

Verticals			
300	37"	American Oak	2,590.
300	37"	Hallmark Cherry	2,590.
100	39"	"MelodyMaker" Polished Ebony (73)	1,790.

*For explanation of terms and prices, please see pages 42–48.

Model	Size	Style and Finish	Price*

Ellington (continued)

Model	Size	Style and Finish	Price*
100	39"	"MelodyMaker" Polished Cherry (73)	1,970.
350	42-1/2"	Continental Polished Ebony	2,790.
350	42-1/2"	Continental Polished Mahogany	2,790.
350	42-1/2"	Continental Polished Cherry	2,790.
310	43"	Vintage Mahogany	2,790.
310	43"	American Oak	2,790.
310	43"	Hallmark Cherry	2,790.
360	47"	Classic Polished Ebony	3,390.
360	47"	Classic Polished Mahogany	3,390.

Grands

Model	Size	Style and Finish	Price*
391	4' 7"	Polished Ebony	7,390.
391	4' 7"	Polished Mahogany	7,790.
391	4' 7"	Polished White	7,390.
396	5' 1"	Polished Ebony	8,790.
396	5' 1"	Polished Mahogany	9,190.
396	5' 1"	Polished White	8,790.

Essex

Verticals

Model	Size	Style and Finish	Price*
EUP-107C	42"	Continental Polished Ebony	5,190.
EUP-111E	44"	European Polished Ebony	5,750.
EUP-111E	44"	European Polished Mahogany	5,890.
EUP-111E	44"	European Polished Walnut	5,930.
EUP-111E	44"	European Polished White	5,790.
EUP-111F	44"	European Cherry	6,270.
EUP-111M	44"	Modern Walnut	5,990.
EUP-111R	44"	English Regency Mahogany	5,830.
EUP-111T	44"	Ash	5,870.

Grands

Model	Size	Style and Finish	Price*
EGP-161	5' 3"	Ebony	14,060.
EGP-161	5' 3"	Polished Ebony	13,790.
EGP-161	5' 3"	Mahogany	15,180.
EGP-161	5' 3"	Polished Mahogany	14,900.
EGP-161	5' 3"	Walnut	15,580.

Model	Size	Style and Finish	Price*
EGP-161	5' 3"	Cherry	15,820.
EGP-161	5' 3"	Oak	15,500.
EGP-161	5' 3"	Polished White	13,960.
EGP-161	5' 3"	Polished Ivory	13,960.
EGP-161N	5' 3"	Neo-Classic Mahogany and Pol. Mahog.	17,500.
EGP-161N	5' 3"	Neo-Classic Cherry	18,500.
EGP-183	6'	Ebony	18,100.
EGP-183	6'	Polished Ebony	17,840.
EGP-183	6'	Polished Mahogany	19,050.
EGP-183	6'	Walnut	19,850.

Estonia

Prices include Jansen adjustable artist bench.

Grands

168	5' 6"	Ebony and Polished Ebony	21,402.
168	5' 6"	Mahogany and Polished Mahogany	23,544.
168	5' 6"	Walnut and Polished Walnut	23,544.
168	5' 6"	*African Bubinga and Pol. Afr. Bubinga*	25,544.
168	5' 6"	*White and Polished White*	24,544.
190	6' 3"	Ebony and Polished Ebony	26,550.
190	6' 3"	Mahogany and Polished Mahogany	29,206.
190	6' 3"	Walnut and Polished Walnut	29,206.
190	6' 3"	*African Bubinga and Pol. Afr. Bubinga*	31,206.
190	6' 3"	*White and Polished White*	30,206.
273	9'	Ebony and Polished Ebony	65,000.

Eterna

Verticals

ERC 10	44"	Continental Polished Ebony	3,690.

Everett

Verticals

EV-111T	44"	Cherry	3,190.
EV-111T	44"	Oak	3,190.

*For explanation of terms and prices, please see pages 42–48.

Model	Size	Style and Finish	Price*

Everett (continued)

Model	Size	Style and Finish	Price*
EV-111F	44"	French Provincial Cherry	3,190.
EV-111F	44"	French Provincial Oak	3,190.
EV-112	44"	Continental Polished Ebony	2,590.
EV-112	44"	Continental Polished Mahogany	2,700.
EV-113	45"	Polished Ebony	2,790.
EV-113	45"	Polished Mahogany	2,900.
EV-115CB	45"	Chippendale Polished Mahogany	3,100.
EV-121	48"	Polished Ebony	3,190.
EV-121	48"	Polished Mahogany	3,300.

Grands

Model	Size	Style and Finish	Price*
EV-152	5'	Polished Ebony	7,780.
EV-152	5'	Polished Mahogany	8,280.
EV-152	5'	Polished Walnut	8,280.
EV-152	5'	Polished White	8,280.
EV-165	5' 5"	Polished Ebony	8,780.
EV-165	5' 5"	Polished Mahogany	9,280.
EV-165	5' 5"	Polished Walnut	9,280.
EV-185	6' 1"	Polished Ebony	10,780.
EV-185	6' 1"	Polished Mahogany	11,380.
EV-185	6' 1"	Polished Walnut	11,380.

Falcone

Verticals

Model	Size	Style and Finish	Price*
UF13MD	44"	Polished Mahogany	3,640.
UF12T	45"	Polished Ebony	3,000.
UF12T	45"	Polished Mahogany	3,060.
UF12T	45"	Polished Walnut	3,060.
UF12T	45"	Polished Ivory	3,060.
UF19FD	47"	Cherry	3,760.
UF19M1D	47"	Oak	3,760.
UF19TD	47"	Polished Ebony	3,240.
UF19TD	47"	Polished Mahogany	3,300.
UF19TD	47"	Polished Walnut	3,300.
UF19TD	47"	Polished Ivory	3,300.

Model	Size	Style and Finish	Price*
UF20TD	48"	Polished Ebony	3,440.
UF20TD	48"	Polished Mahogany	3,500.
UF20TD	48"	Polished Walnut	3,500.
UF20TD	48"	Polished Ivory	3,500.
UF23FD	49"	Queen Anne Polished Mahogany	3,660.
UF23TD	49"	Polished Ebony	3,600.
UF23TD	49"	Polished Mahogany	3,660.
UF23TD	49"	Polished Walnut	3,660.
UF32TD	52"	Polished Ebony	3,720.
UF32TD	52"	Polished Mahogany	3,720.
UF32TD	52"	Polished Walnut	3,720.
Grands			
GF52D	5'	Polished Ebony	9,080.
GF52D	5'	Polished Mahogany	9,280.
GF52D	5'	Polished Walnut	9,280.
GF52D	5'	Polished Ivory	9,180.
GF52FD	5'	French Polished Mahogany	9,580.
GF52FD	5'	French Polished Red Oak	9,580.
GF52FD	5'	French Polished Ivory	9,480.
GF62D	5' 4"	Polished Ebony	10,040.
GF62D	5' 4"	Polished Mahogany	10,240.
GF62D	5' 4"	Polished Walnut	10,240.
GF62D	5' 4"	Polished Ivory	10,140.
GF72D	5' 8"	Polished Ebony	10,720.
GF72D	5' 8"	Polished Mahogany	10,920.
GF72D	5' 8"	Polished Walnut	10,920.
GF72D	5' 8"	Polished Ivory	10,820.
GF72D-LXV	5' 8"	Louis XV Polished Ebony	10,960.
GF72D-LXV	5' 8"	Louis XV Mahogany	11,160.
GF72DF	5' 8"	French Provincial Polished Mahogany	11,220.
GF72DF	5' 8"	French Provincial Polished Ivory	11,120.
GF87D	6' 2"	Polished Ebony	11,680.
GF87D	6' 2"	Polished Mahogany	11,880.
GF87D	6' 2"	Polished Walnut	11,780.
GF87D-LXV	6' 2"	Polished Ebony	11,680.
GF87D-LXV	6' 2"	Polished Mahogany	11,880.
GF87D-LXV	6' 2"	Polished Ivory	11,780.

*For explanation of terms and prices, please see pages 42–48.

Fazioli

Fazioli is willing to make custom-designed cases with exotic veneers, marquetry, and other embellishments. Prices on request to Fazioli.

Grands

Model	Size	Style and Finish	Price
F156	5' 2"	Ebony and Polished Ebony	75,700.
F156	5' 2"	Walnut	78,600.
F156	5' 2"	Polished Walnut	81,100.
F156	5' 2"	Polished Pyramid Mahogany	83,600.
F156	5' 2"	Cherry	78,600.
F156	5' 2"	Polished Cherry	81,100.
F183	6'	Ebony and Polished Ebony	84,400.
F183	6'	Walnut	88,300.
F183	6'	Polished Walnut	90,600.
F183	6'	Polished Pyramid Mahogany	93,700.
F183	6'	Cherry	88,300.
F183	6'	Polished Cherry	90,600.
F212	6' 11"	Ebony and Polished Ebony	95,000.
F212	6' 11"	Walnut	99,000.
F212	6' 11"	Polished Walnut	101,700.
F212	6' 11"	Polished Pyramid Mahogany	105,100.
F212	6' 11"	Cherry	99,000.
F212	6' 11"	Polished Cherry	101,700.
F228	7' 6"	Ebony and Polished Ebony	107,000.
F228	7' 6"	Walnut	111,300.
F228	7' 6"	Polished Walnut	113,800.
F228	7' 6"	Polished Pyramid Mahogany	119,200.
F228	7' 6"	Cherry	111,300.
F228	7' 6"	Polished Cherry	113,800.
F278	9' 2"	Ebony and Polished Ebony	136,600.
F278	9' 2"	Walnut	142,200.
F278	9' 2"	Polished Walnut	146,500.
F278	9' 2"	Polished Pyramid Mahogany	151,400.
F278	9' 2"	Cherry	142,200.
F278	9' 2"	Polished Cherry	146,500.
F308	10' 2"	Ebony and Polished Ebony	174,000.
F308	10' 2"	Walnut	181,600.

Model	Size	Style and Finish	Price*
F308	10' 2"	Polished Walnut	184,000.
F308	10' 2"	Polished Pyramid Mahogany	189,600.
F308	10' 2"	Cherry	181,600.
F308	10' 2"	Polished Cherry	184,000.
All models		*Fourth Pedal, add'l*	6,200.
All models		*Third and Fourth Pedals (set), add'l*	7,700.
All models		*Magnetic Balanced Action, add'l*	8,500.

Feurich

Prices are F.O.B. Germany and do not include bench.

Grands

F 172	5' 8"	Polished Ebony	44,290.
F 172	5' 8"	Classic French Polished Ebony	50,860.
F 172	5' 8"	Rococo	80,080.
F 222	7' 3"	Polished Ebony	69,000.
F 222	7' 3"	Classic French Polished Ebony	75,210.

Förster, August

Prices do not include bench. Although prices include estimated duty and shipping, because dealers purchase directly from the manufacturer, actual price at time of sale may vary depending on the value of the Euro, the dealer's location, and the shipping method utilized. The prices below were calculated at Euro=$1.11.

Verticals

116C	46"	Chippendale Polished Ebony	17,303.
116C	46"	Chippendale Walnut and Pol. Walnut	18,119.
116C	46"	Chippendale Mahog. and Pol. Mahog.	17,373.
116C	46"	Chippendale Polished White	17,688.
116D	46"	Continental Polished Ebony	14,692.
116D	46"	Continental Walnut and Pol. Walnut	15,566.
116D	46"	Continental Mahog.and Pol. Mahog.	14,739.
116D	46"	Continental Polished White	15,089.
116E	46"	Polished Ebony	17,303.
116E	46"	Walnut and Polished Walnut	18,119.
116E	46"	Mahogany and Polished Mahogany	17,373.

*For explanation of terms and prices, please see pages 42–48.

Model	Size	Style and Finish	Price*

Förster, August (continued)

Model	Size	Style and Finish	Price*
116E	46"	Polished White	17,688.
125G	49"	Polished Ebony	18,573.
125G	49"	Walnut and Polished Walnut	19,471.
125G	49"	Mahogany and Polished Mahogany	18,632.
125G	49"	Polished White	18,970.
Grands			
170	5' 8"	Polished Ebony	38,149.
170	5' 8"	Walnut and Polished Walnut	39,489.
170	5' 8"	Mahogany and Polished Mahogany	38,219.
170	5' 8"	Polished White	39,793.
170	5' 8"	*Pyramid Mahogany*	43,510.
170	5' 8"	"Classic" Polished Ebony	42,543.
170	5' 8"	"Classic" Walnut and Polished Walnut	48,289.
170	5' 8"	"Classic" Mahogany and Pol.Mahogany	43,336.
170	5' 8"	"Classic" Polished White	45,830.
170	5' 8"	*Chippendale, additional*	8,800.
190	6' 4"	Polished Ebony	43,207.
190	6' 4"	Walnut and Polished Walnut	44,653.
190	6' 4"	Mahogany and Polished Mahogany	43,359.
190	6' 4"	Polished White	44,909.
190	6' 4"	*Pyramid Mahogany*	48,568.
190	6' 4"	"Classic" Polished Ebony	47,601.
190	6' 4"	"Classic" Walnut and Polished Walnut	53,452.
190	6' 4"	"Classic" Mahogany and Pol.Mahogany	48,475.
190	6' 4"	"Classic" Polished White	50,946.
190	6' 4"	*Chippendale, additional*	8,800.
215	7' 2"	Polished Ebony	49,455.
275	9' 1"	Polished Ebony	93,207.

Grotrian

Prices do not include bench.

Verticals

Model	Size	Style and Finish	Price*
Caret	44"	Polished Ebony	19,000.
Caret	44"	Polished Walnut	20,000.

Model	Size	Style and Finish	Price*
Caret	44"	Polished Mahogany	20,000.
Classic	49"	Polished Ebony	23,800.
Classic	49"	Polished Walnut	25,400.
Classic	49"	Polished Mahogany	25,400.
Concertino	52"	Polished Ebony	27,200.
Grands			
Chambre	5' 5"	Ebony	44,600.
Chambre	5' 5"	Polished Ebony	49,000.
Chambre	5' 5"	Polished Walnut	53,800.
Cabinet	6' 3"	Ebony	49,400.
Cabinet	6' 3"	Polished Ebony	54,000.
Cabinet	6' 3"	Polished Walnut	58,000.
Concert	7' 4"	Ebony	60,800.
Concert	7' 4"	Polished Ebony	65,000.
Concert Royal	9' 2"	Polished Ebony	75,400.

Haessler

Prices do not include bench.

Verticals

Model	Size	Style and Finish	Price
115 K	45"	Ebony and Polished Ebony	13,780.
115 K	45"	Waxed Alder	13,506.
115 K	45"	Beech	13,506.
115 K	45"	Ash	13,506.
115 K	45"	White and Polished White	14,400.
118 K	47"	Ebony and Polished Ebony	15,414.
118 K	47"	Ebony with Walnut Accent	16,680.
118 K	47"	Mahogany and Polished Mahogany	16,242.
118 K	47"	Walnut and Polished Walnut	16,242.
118 K	47"	Cherry and Polished Cherry	16,704.
118 K	47"	Cherry with Yew Inlay, Satin and Polish	17,622.
118 K	47"	Oak	14,564.
118 K	47"	White and Polished White	16,058.
118 KM	47"	Ebony and Polished Ebony	16,334.
118 KM	47"	White and Polished White	17,024.
118 CH	47"	Chippendale Mahogany and Pol.Mahog.	17,622.
118 CH	47"	Chippendale Walnut and Pol. Walnut	18,014.

*For explanation of terms and prices, please see pages 42–48.

Model	Size	Style and Finish	Price*

Haessler (continued)

Model	Size	Style and Finish	Price*
124 K	49"	Ebony and Polished Ebony	16,520.
124 K	49"	Ebony with Walnut Accent	17,462.
124 K	49"	Mahogany and Polished Mahogany	17,898.
124 K	49"	Walnut and Polished Walnut	17,898.
124 K	49"	Cherry and Polished Cherry	18,426.
124 K	49"	Cherry with Yew Inlay, Satin and Polish	19,348.
124 K	49"	White and Polished White	17,208.
124 KM	49"	Ebony and Polished Ebony	17,160.
124 KM	49"	White and Polished White	17,160.
132	52"	Ebony and Polished Ebony	23,254.
Grands			
175	5' 8"	Ebony and Polished Ebony	42,346.
175	5' 8"	Mahogany and Polished Mahogany	45,744.
175	5' 8"	Saxony Polished Pyramid Mahogany	57,180.
175	5' 8"	Walnut and Polished Walnut	46,184.
175	5' 8"	Saxony Polished Burl Walnut	57,728.
175	5' 8"	Cherry and Polished Cherry	45,962.
175	5' 8"	Polished Bubinga	48,382.
175	5' 8"	White and Polished White	44,464.
186	6' 1"	Ebony and Polished Ebony	47,710.
186	6' 1"	Mahogany and Polished Mahogany	51,536.
186	6' 1"	Saxony Polished Pyramid Mahogany	64,424.
186	6' 1"	Walnut and Polished Walnut	52,034.
186	6' 1"	Saxony Polished Burl Walnut	65,040.
186	6' 1"	Cherry and Polished Cherry	51,784.
186	6' 1"	Polished Bubinga	54,512.
186	6' 1"	White and Polished White	50,096.

Hallet, Davis & Co

Model	Size	Style and Finish	Price*
Verticals			
H-C43F	43"	French Oak	2,990.
H-C43F	43"	French Mahogany	2,990.
H-C43F	43"	French Cherry	2,990.
H-C43R	43"	Oak (round leg)	2,990.

Model	Size	Style and Finish	Price*
H-C43R	43"	Mahogany (round leg)	2,990.
H-111GD	44"	Continental Polished Ebony	2,500.
H-111GD	44"	Continental Polished Mahogany	2,550.
H-111GD	44"	Continental Polished Walnut	2,550.
H-111GD	44"	Continental Polished White	2,550.
H-115GC	45"	Chippendale Polished Ebony	2,750.
H-115GC	45"	Chippendale Polished Mahogany	2,790.
H-115GC	45"	Chippendale Polished Brown Mahogany	2,790.
H-115WH	46"	Polished Ebony	2,790.
H-115WH	46"	Polished Mahogany	2,840.
H-115WH	46"	Polished Walnut	2,840.
H-121WH	48"	Polished Ebony	2,990.
H-121WH	48"	Polished Mahogany	3,100.
H-121WH	48"	Polished Walnut	3,100.
HU-131X	52"	Polished Ebony	3,990.
HU-131X	52"	Polished Mahogany	3,990.
Grands			
H-143	4' 7"	Polished Ebony	6,390.
H-143	4' 7"	Polished Mahogany	6,790.
H-143	4' 7"	Polished Walnut	6,790.
H-143F	4' 7"	Queen Anne Polished Ebony	7,190.
H-143F	4' 7"	Queen Anne Polished Mahogany	7,190.
H-143F	4' 7"	Queen Anne Polished Walnut	7,190.
H-152C	5'	Polished Ebony	7,990.
H-152C	5'	Polished Mahogany	8,390.
H-152C	5'	Polished Walnut	8,390.
H-152C	5'	Polished White	8,390.
H-152D	5'	Polished Ebony	8,590.
H-152D	5'	Polished Mahogany	8,990.
H-152D	5'	Polished Walnut	8,990.
H-152S	5'	Queen Anne Polished Mahogany	8,990.
HDG-480	5' 1"	Polished Ebony	9,770.
HDG-480	5' 1"	Polished Mahogany	10,110.
H-165C	5' 5"	Polished Ebony	8,790.
H-165C	5' 5"	Polished Mahogany	9,190.
H-165C	5' 5"	Polished Walnut	9,190.
H-165C	5' 5"	Polished White	9,190.

*For explanation of terms and prices, please see pages 42–48.

Model	Size	Style and Finish	Price*

Hallet, Davis & Co. (continued)

Model	Size	Style and Finish	Price
H-165D	5' 5"	Polished Mahogany	9,790.
H-185C	6' 1"	Polished Ebony	10,790.
H-185C	6' 1"	Polished Mahogany	11,190.
H-185C	6' 1"	Polished Walnut	11,190.

Hayden

Verticals

Model	Size	Style and Finish	Price
UP-110GD	43"	Cherry	2,990.
UP-110GE	43"	Mahogany	3,190.
114RPN	45"	Polished Dark Walnut	3,190.
115FM	45-1/2"	Mahogany	3,190.
115OS	45-1/2"	Light Cherry	3,190.
115GC	45-1/2"	Polished Mahogany	3,390.
121RP	48"	Polished Ebony	3,390.

Grands

Model	Size	Style and Finish	Price
G-152	5'	Polished Ebony	7,790.
G-165	5' 6"	Polished Ebony	8,790.
G-185	6' 1"	Polished Ebony	10,580.

Hyundai

Verticals

Model	Size	Style and Finish	Price
U-800	42"	Continental Polished Ebony	3,998.
U-800	42"	Continental Walnut	3,758.
U-800	42"	Continental Polished Mahogany	4,300.
U-800	42"	Continental Polished White	4,300.
U-800	42"	Continental Polished Ivory	3,998.
U-824F	43"	French Walnut	4,998.
U-824F	43"	French Brown Oak	4,998.
U-824F	43"	French Cherry	4,998.
U-824M	43"	Mediterranean Brown Oak	4,998.
U-824M	43"	Mediterranean Walnut	4,998.
U-824M	43"	Mediterranean Cherry	4,998.
U-842	46"	Chippendale Polished Mahogany	5,598.

Model	Size	Style and Finish	Price*
U-852	46"	Ebony and Polished Ebony	5,598.
U-852	46"	Brown Oak	5,598.
U-852	46"	Walnut	5,198.
U-860E	46"	Cherry	5,398
U-860E	46"	Walnut	5,398
U-832	48"	Ebony and Polished Ebony	5,198.
U-832	48"	Walnut and Polished Walnut	5,398.
U-832	48"	Brown Oak	5,398.
U-832	48"	Polished Mahogany	5,398.
U-837	52"	Ebony	5,598.
U-837	52"	Polished Ebony	5,698.
U-837	52"	Walnut	5,598.
U-837	52"	Polished Walnut	5,798.
U-837	52"	Polished Mahogany	5,798.
Grands			
G-50A	4' 7"	Ebony	9,898.
G-50A	4' 7"	Polished Ebony	9,998.
G-50A	4' 7"	Walnut and Polished Walnut	10,398.
G-50A	4' 7"	Polished Mahogany	10,398.
G-50A	4' 7"	Brown Oak and Polished Brown Oak	10,398.
G-50A	4' 7"	Cherry	10,398.
G-50A	4' 7"	Polished Ivory	10,198.
G-50A	4' 7"	Polished White	10,198.
G-50AF	4' 7"	Queen Anne Walnut and Pol. Walnut	11,900.
G-50AF	4' 7"	Queen Anne Polished Mahogany	11,900.
G-50AF	4' 7"	Queen Anne Oak and Polished Oak	11,900.
G-50AF	4' 7"	Queen Anne Cherry	11,900.
G-50AF	4' 7"	Queen Anne Polished White	11,900.
G-50AF	4' 7"	Queen Anne Polished Ivory	11,900.
G-80A	5' 1"	Ebony	11,398.
G-80A	5' 1"	Polished Ebony	11,498.
G-80A	5' 1"	Walnut and Polished Walnut	11,898.
G-80A	5' 1"	Polished Mahogany	11,898.
G-80A	5' 1"	Brown Oak and Polished Brown Oak	11,898.
G-80A	5' 1"	Cherry	11,898.
G-80A	5' 1"	Polished Ivory	11,698.
G-80A	5' 1"	Polished White	11,698.

*For explanation of terms and prices, please see pages 42–48.

| --- | --- | --- | --- |

Hyundai (continued)

G-80AF	5' 1"	Queen Anne Polished Mahogany	14,098.
G-80B	5' 1"	Chippendale Polished Mahogany	14,098.
G-81	5' 9"	Chippendale Polished Mahogany	15,398.
G-82	5' 9"	Ebony	12,798.
G-82	5' 9"	Polished Ebony	12,898.
G-82	5' 9"	Walnut and Polished Walnut	13,298.
G-82	5' 9"	Polished Mahogany	13,298.
G-82	5' 9"	Polished White	13,098.
G-82AF	5' 9"	Queen Anne Polished Mahogany	15,398.
G-84	6' 1"	Ebony	13,498.
G-84	6' 1"	Polished Ebony	13,598.
G-84	6' 1"	Walnut and Polished Walnut	13,998.
G-84	6' 1"	Polished Mahogany	13,998.
G-85	6' 10"	Ebony and Polished Ebony	17,398.

Ibach

Prices vary with the value of the Dollar against the Euro. These prices were computed with Euro=$1.15. Prices are F.O.B. Las Vegas.

Verticals

B-114	45"	"Classic/Tradition" Open-Pore Beech	16,056.
B-114	45"	"Classic/Tradition" Open-Pore Alder	16,056.
B-114	45"	"Classic/Tradition" Open-Pore Oak	16,056.
B-114	45"	"Classic/Tradition" Open-Pore Maple	16,402.
B-114	45"	"Classic/Tradition" Open-Pore Cherry	16,402.
C-118	46-1/2"	"Elegance" Open-Pore Beech	17,302.
C-118	46-1/2"	"Elegance" Open-Pore Oak	17,302.
C-118	46-1/2"	"Elegance" Open-Pore Cherry	17,691.
C-118	46-1/2"	"Elegance" Polished Ebony	17,746.
C-118	46-1/2"	"Elegance" Polished White	18,357.
C-118	46-1/2"	"Elegance" Polished Walnut	19,081.
C-118	46-1/2"	"Elegance" Polished Mahogany	19,081.
C-118	46-1/2"	"Elegance" Polished Cherry	19,081.
C-118	46-1/2"	"Elegance" Polished Burr Walnut	21,138.
C-118	46-1/2"	"Edition (Bruno Paul 1911)" Pol. Ebony	20,749.

Model	Size	Style and Finish	Price*
C-118	46-1/2"	"Edition (Bruno Paul 1911)" Pol. White	21,501.
C-118	46-1/2"	"Edition (Bruno Paul1911)" Oiled Oak	21,501.
C-118	46-1/2"	"Antik" Polished Ebony	on request
K-125	49"	"Exclusive" Polished Ebony	on request
H-128	50"	"Edition" Swiss Pear-Tree	on request
L-132	52"	"Tradition" Polished Ebony	24,974.
Grands			
F-II 183	6'	Polished Ebony	51,492.
F-II 183	6'	Polished Mahogany	56,996.
F-II 183	6'	Polished Burr Walnut	58,374.
F-II 183	6'	*"Edition Ibach Design 1913"*	53,971.
F-II 183	6'	*"Eigenentwurf Ibach Design 1980"*	53,360.
F-II 183	6'	*"Ausfuhrung Art Design"*	64,086.
F-III 215	7' 1"	"Richard Strauss" Polished Ebony	65,228.
F-III 215	7' 1"	*"Klassizismus"*	110,944.
F-III 215	7' 1"	*"Richard Meier"*	on request
F-IV 240	7' 10-1/2"	"Richard Wagner" Polished Ebony	71,078.

Irmler

Verticals

Model	Size	Style and Finish	Price*
M113E	44"	Polished Ebony	7,036.
M113E	44"	Walnut	6,954.
M113E	44"	Polished Walnut	7,300.
M113E	44"	Mahogany	7,126.
M113E	44"	Polished Mahogany	7,300.
M113E	44"	Cherry	7,126.
M113E	44"	Polished Cherry	7,300.
M113E	44"	Beech	6,954.
M113E	44"	Alder	6,954.
M113E	44"	Polished White	7,650.
M122E	49"	Polished Ebony	7,526.
M122E	49"	Walnut	7,476.
M122E	49"	Polished Walnut	7,650.
M122E	49"	Mahogany	7,650.
M122E	49"	Polished Mahogany	7,824.
M122E	49"	Cherry	7,650.

*For explanation of terms and prices, please see pages 42–48.

Model	Size	Style and Finish	Price*

Irmler (continued)

Model	Size	Style and Finish	Price*
M122E	49"	Polished Cherry	7,824.
M122E	49"	Beech	7,300.
M122E	49"	Alder	7,300.
M122E	49"	Polished White	8,170.

Grands

Model	Size	Style and Finish	Price*
F16E	5' 7"	Polished Ebony	23,240.
F16E	5' 7"	Walnut	24,080.
F16E	5' 7"	Polished Walnut	24,640.
F16E	5' 7"	Mahogany	24,080.
F16E	5' 7"	Polished Mahogany	24,640.
F16E	5' 7"	Cherry	24,080.
F16E	5' 7"	Polished Cherry	25,200.
F16E	5' 7"	Polished White	24,360.
F18E	6' 1"	Polished Ebony	25,920.
F18E	6' 1"	Walnut	26,760.
F18E	6' 1"	Polished Walnut	27,320.
F18E	6' 1"	Mahogany	26,760.
F18E	6' 1"	Polished Mahogany	27,320.
F18E	6' 1"	Cherry	27,320.
F18E	6' 1"	Polished Cherry	27,880.
F18E	6' 1"	Polished White	27,040.
F18E	6' 1"	"Classic" Polished Ebony	29,400.
F18E	6' 1"	"Classic" Polished Walnut	30,520.
F18E	6' 1"	"Classic" Polished Mahogany	30,520.
F18E	6' 1"	"Classic" Polished Cherry	31,080.
F18E	6' 1"	Chippendale Polished Ebony	29,400.
F18E	6' 1"	Chippendale Polished Walnut	30,800.
F18E	6' 1"	Chippendale Polished Mahogany	30,800.
F18E	6' 1"	Chippendale Polished White	30,800.
F122E	7'	Polished Ebony	36,600.
F122E	7'	Polished Walnut	39,400.
F122E	7'	Polished Mahogany	39,400.
F122E	7'	Polished Cherry	39,400.
F122E	7'	Polished White	38,000.

Model	Size	Style and Finish	Price*

Kawai

Verticals

Model	Size	Style and Finish	Price*
K-18	44-1/2"	Polished Ebony	4,590.
K-18	44-1/2"	Polished Mahogany	5,190.
506N	44-1/2"	Mahogany	3,590.
506N	44-1/2"	Oak	3,590.
508	44-1/2"	Mahogany	4,190.
508	44-1/2"	Oak	4,190.
606	44-1/2"	Oak	4,490.
606	44-1/2"	French Provincial Cherry	4,690.
606	44-1/2"	Queen Anne Mahogany	4,790.
606	45"	Queen Anne Cherry	5,990.
606	45"	Spanish Provincial Oak	5,890.
UST-7	46"	Ebony	6,690.
UST-7	46"	Oak	6,690.
UST-7	46"	Walnut	6,690.
UST-8	46"	Ebony	5,590.
UST-8	46"	Walnut	5,590.
UST-8	46"	Oak	5,590.
906	46-1/2"	Country Manor Oak	7,090.
906	46-1/2"	English Regency Mahogany	7,190.
906	46-1/2"	French Provincial Cherry	7,190.
UST-10	48"	Ebony	7,790.
UST-10	48"	Mahogany	7,790.
K-25	48"	Ebony	5,990.
K-25	48"	Polished Ebony	5,590.
K-25	48"	Mahogany and Polished Mahogany	6,190.
K-25	48"	Polished Snow White	5,990.
K-50	49"	Ebony and Polished Ebony	7,790.
K-50	49"	Polished Sapeli Mahogany	8,990.
K-50	49"	Walnut	8,590.
K-50	49"	Polished Walnut	8,990.
K-60	52"	Ebony and Polished Ebony	10,490.
K-80	52"	Ebony and Polished Ebony	12,590.

*For explanation of terms and prices, please see pages 42–48.

Kawai (continued)

Grands

Model	Size	Style and Finish	Price*
GM-10	5'	Ebony	12,290.
GM-10	5'	Polished Ebony	12,390.
GM-10	5'	Polished Mahogany	13,590.
GM-10	5'	Polished Snow White	13,590.
GM-10F	5'	French Provincial Polished Mahogany	14,590.
GE-20	5' 1"	Ebony	14,490.
GE-20	5' 1"	Polished Ebony	14,890.
GE-20	5' 1"	Walnut	16,390.
GE-20	5' 1"	Mahogany	16,190.
GE-20	5' 1"	Polished Mahogany	16,590.
GE-20	5' 1"	Polished Sapeli Mahogany	16,590.
GE-20	5' 1"	Polished Snow White	15,990.
GE-20F	5' 1"	French Provincial Polished Mahogany	17,990.
GE-30	5' 5"	Ebony	16,390.
GE-30	5' 5"	Polished Ebony	16,590.
GE-30	5' 5"	Mahogany	18,290.
GE-30	5' 5"	Polished Mahogany	18,490.
GE-30	5' 5"	Polished Sapeli Mahogany	18,290.
GE-30	5' 5"	Polished Snow White	17,590.
RX-1	5' 5"	Ebony	18,590.
RX-1	5' 5"	Polished Ebony	18,990.
RX-1	5' 5"	Walnut	20,370.
RX-1	5' 5"	Polished Walnut	20,990.
RX-1	5' 5"	Polished Sapeli Mahogany	20,590.
RX-1	5' 5"	Polished Snow White	19,790.
RX-2	5' 10"	Ebony	21,390.
RX-2	5' 10"	Polished Ebony	21,590.
RX-2	5' 10"	Walnut	23,190.
RX-2	5' 10"	Polished Walnut	24,390.
RX-2	5' 10"	Polished Mahogany	23,190.
RX-2	5' 10"	Polished Sapeli Mahogany	23,390.
RX-2	5' 10"	Oak	22,190.
RX-2	5' 10"	Cherry	23,190.
RX-2	5' 10"	Polished Rosewood	27,590.

Model	Size	Style and Finish	Price*
RX-2	5' 10"	Polished Snow White	22,590.
RX-2F	5' 10"	French Provincial Polished Mahogany	27,390.
RX-3	6' 1"	Ebony	27,390.
RX-3	6' 1"	Polished Ebony	27,990.
RX-3	6' 1"	Walnut	29,990.
RX-3	6' 1"	Polished Sapeli Mahogany	30,590.
RX-3	6' 1"	Polished Snow White	28,990.
CR40N	6' 1"	Plexiglass	75,260.
RX-5	6' 6"	Ebony	30,990.
RX-5	6' 6"	Polished Ebony	31,190.
RX-5	6' 6"	Walnut	33,990.
RX-5	6' 6"	Polished Sapeli Mahogany	33,990.
RX-5	6' 6"	Polished Snow White	32,590.
RX-6	7'	Ebony	34,790.
RX-6	7'	Polished Ebony	34,990.
RX-7	7' 6"	Ebony	39,790.
RX-7	7' 6"	Polished Ebony	40,190.
RX-7	7' 6"	Polished Rosewood	46,790.
GS-100	9' 1"	Ebony	77,990.
GS-100	9' 1"	Polished Ebony	79,990.
EX	9' 1"	Polished Ebony	109,190.
EX-G	9' 1"	Polished Ebony	115,990.

Kawai, Shigeru

Grands

SK2	5' 10"	Polished Ebony	38,390.
SK2	5' 10"	Polished Sapeli Mahogany	40,590.
SK3	6' 1"	Polished Ebony	44,990.
SK3	6' 1"	Polished Sapeli Mahogany	47,190.
SK5	6' 6"	Polished Ebony	51,590.
SK5	6' 6"	Polished Sapeli Mahogany	54,890.
SK6	7'	Polished Ebony	58,190.
SK7	7' 6"	Polished Ebony	64,790.

*For explanation of terms and prices, please see pages 42–48.

Model	Size	Style and Finish	Price*

Kemble

Verticals

Oxford	43"	Polished Ebony	7,660.
Oxford	43"	Mahogany	6,940.
Oxford	43"	Georgian Mahogany Lustre	7,660.
Oxford	43"	Polished Mahogany	7,660.
Oxford	43"	Polished Walnut	7,660.
Oxford	43"	Beech	7,660.
Classic-T	45"	Polished Ebony	8,000.
Classic-T	45"	Polished Ebony and Chrome	8,280.
Empire	46-1/2"	Empire Polished Mahogany	9,740.
Prestige	46-1/2"	Cherry with Yew Inlay	9,740.
Windsor	46-1/2"	Polished Ebony with Burr Walnut	8,900.
Windsor	46-1/2"	Georgian Mahogany Lustre	8,700.
Windsor	46-1/2"	Polished Mahogany	8,700.
K121ZT	48"	Polished Ebony	9,740.
K121ZT	48"	Georgian Mahogany Lustre	9,540.
K121ZT	48"	Polished Mahogany	9,740.
K121ZT	48"	Polished Walnut	9,740.
Vermont	48"	Cherry	11,400.
K131	52"	Polished Ebony	13,080.
K131	52"	Polished Mahogany	13,080.

Grands

KC 173	5' 8"	Polished Ebony	23,800.

Knabe, Wm.

Verticals

WKV-118F	46-1/2"	French Provincial Polished Mahogany	6,940.
WKV-118F	46-1/2"	French Provincial Polished Cherry	6,940.
WKV-118F	46-1/2"	French Provincial Polished Oak	6,940.
WKV-118R	46-1/2"	Renaissance Ebony	6,940.
WKV-118R	46-1/2"	Renaissance Polished Walnut	6,940.
WKV-118R	46-1/2"	Renaissance Polished Oak	6,940.
WKV-118T	46-1/2"	Polished Mahogany	6,940.

Model	Size	Style and Finish	Price*
WKV-118T	46-1/2"	Polished Cherry	6,940.
WKV-121D	48"	Ebony and Polished Ebony	6,940.
WKV-131MD	52"	Ebony	7,740.
WKV-131MD	52"	Polished Ebony	7,540.

Grands

Model	Size	Style and Finish	Price*
WKG-53	5' 3"	Ebony and Polished Ebony	16,940.
WKG-53	5' 3"	Semi-Gloss Mahogany	19,340.
WKG-53	5' 3"	Semi-Gloss Walnut	19,340.
WKG-53	5' 3"	Semi-Gloss Cherry	19,340.
WKG-53KBF	5' 3"	French Prov. Semi-Gloss Mahogany	23,850.
WKG-53KBF	5' 3"	French Provincial Semi-Gloss Walnut	23,850.
WKG-53KBF	5' 3"	French Provincial Semi-Gloss Cherry	23,850.
WKG-53M	5' 3"	Empire Ebony and Polished Ebony	19,340.
WKG-53M	5' 3"	Empire Semi-Gloss Mahogany	21,340.
WKG-53M	5' 3"	Empire Semi-Gloss Walnut	21,340.
WKG-53M	5' 3"	Empire Semi-Gloss Cherry	21,340.
WKG-57	5' 7"	Ebony and Polished Ebony	23,350.
WKG-57	5' 7"	Semi-Gloss Mahogany	25,350.
WKG-57	5' 7"	Semi-Gloss Walnut	25,350.
WKG-57	5' 7"	Semi-Gloss Cherry	25,350.
WKG-61	6' 1"	Ebony and Polished Ebony	24,340.
WKG-61	6' 1"	Semi-Gloss Mahogany	26,340.
WKG-61	6' 1"	Semi-Gloss Walnut	26,340.
WKG-61	6' 1"	Semi-Gloss Cherry	26,340.
WKG-61L	6' 1"	Empire Semi-Gloss Mahogany	27,250.
WKG-61L	6' 1"	Empire Semi-Gloss Walnut	27,250.
WKG-61L	6' 1"	Empire Semi-Gloss Cherry	27,250.
WKG-64	6' 4"	Ebony	28,250.
WKG-64	6' 4"	Semi-Gloss Mahogany	30,250.
WKG-64	6' 4"	Semi-Gloss Walnut	30,250.
WKG-68	6' 8"	Ebony and Polished Walnut	26,340.
WKG-68	6' 8"	Semi-Gloss Mahogany	28,340.
WKG-68	6' 8"	Semi-Gloss Walnut	28,340.
WKG-70	7'	Ebony and Polished Ebony	29,350.

*For explanation of terms and prices, please see pages 42–48.

Kohler & Campbell

In general, "Wood Finishes" means mahogany, walnut, cherry, and brown oak. However, even where not specifically indicated, most models are available by special order in any finish.

Verticals

Model	Size	Style and Finish	Price
KC-142	42"	Continental Ebony	3,140.
KC-142	42"	Continental Polished Ebony	3,040.
KC-142	42"	Continental Satin/Pol. Wood Finishes	3,140.
KC-142	42"	Continental Polished Ivory/White	3,140.
KC-244F	44"	French Provincial Wood Finishes	3,840.
KC-244M	44"	Mediterranean Wood Finishes	3,740.
KC-244T	44"	Wood Finishes	3,840.
KC-245	45"	Ebony	3,340.
KC-245	45"	Polished Ebony	3,240.
KC-245	45"	Satin/Polished Wood Finishes	3,340.
KC-245	45"	Polished Ivory/White	3,340.
KC-247	46-1/2"	Ebony and Polished Ebony	4,940.
KC-247	46-1/2"	Satin/Polished Wood Finishes	4,940.
KC-647F	46-1/2"	French Provincial Wood Finishes	4,440.
KC-647R	46-1/2"	Renaissance Wood Finishes	4,240.
KC-647T	46-1/2"	Wood Finishes	4,440.
KMV-47F	46-1/2"	"Millennium" Fr. Prov. Semi-Gloss Wood	6,540.
KMV-47T	46-1/2"	"Millennium" Semi-gloss Wood Finish	6,540.
KC-121F	48"	French Provincial Ebony	4,540.
KC-121F	48"	French Provincial Polished Ebony	4,340.
KC-121F	48"	French Provincial Satin/Pol. Wood Fin.	4,540.
KC-121M	48"	Mediterranean Ebony	4,540.
KC-121M	48"	Mediterranean Polished Ebony	4,260.
KC-121M	48"	Mediterranean Satin/Pol. Wood Finishes	4,540.
KMV-48SD	48"	"Millennium" Ebony	7,740.
KMV-48SD	48"	"Millennium" Polished Ebony	6,340.
KMV-48SD	48"	"Millennium" Polished Wood Finishes	7,740.
KMV-52MD	52"	"Millennium" Ebony	8,220.
KMV-52MD	52"	"Millennium" Polished Ebony	6,940.
KMV-52MD	52"	"Millennium" Polished Wood Finishes	8,220.

Model	Size	Style and Finish	Price*
Grands			
KIG-47	4' 7"	Ebony	8,440.
KIG-47	4' 7"	Polished Ebony	8,040.
KIG-47	4' 7"	Polished Mahogany	8,440.
KIG-47	4' 7"	Polished Walnut	8,440.
KIG-47	4' 7"	Polished Ivory/White	8,440.
KIG-52	5' 1-1/2"	Ebony	9,940.
KIG-52	5' 1-1/2"	Polished Ebony	9,540.
KIG-52	5' 1-1/2"	Polished Mahogany	9,940.
KIG-52	5' 1-1/2"	Polished Walnut	9,940.
KIG-52	5' 1-1/2"	Polished Ivory/White	9,940.
SKG-530S	5' 2"	Ebony	13,340.
SKG-530S	5' 2"	Polished Ebony	12,340.
SKG-530S	5' 2"	Satin/Polished Wood Finishes	13,340.
SKG-530S	5' 2"	Polished Ivory/White	13,340.
SKG-530SM	5' 2"	Empire Polished Mahogany	14,140.
SKG-530SM	5' 2"	Empire Polished Walnut	14,140.
SKG-530SM	5' 2"	Empire Polished Ivory/White	14,140.
SKG-530SKBF	5' 2"	French Provincial Polished Mahogany	15,340.
SKG-530SKBF	5' 2"	French Provincial Polished Walnut	15,340.
SKG-530SKBF	5' 2"	French Provincial Polished Ivory/White	15,340.
SKG-600S	5' 9"	Ebony	14,140.
SKG-600S	5' 9"	Polished Ebony	13,540.
SKG-600S	5' 9"	Satin/Polished Wood Finishes	14,140.
SKG-600S	5' 9"	Polished Ivory/White	14,140.
SKG-600SL	5' 9"	Empire Ebony	15,140.
SKG-600SL	5' 9"	Empire Polished Ebony	14,540.
SKG-600SL	5' 9"	Empire Satin/Polished Wood Finishes	15,140.
SKG-600SL	5' 9"	Empire Polished Ivory/White	15,140.
KFM-600S	5' 9"	"Millennium" Ebony	21,740.
KFM-600S	5' 9"	"Millennium" Polished Ebony	21,340.
KFM-600S	5' 9"	"Millennium" Semi-Gloss Wood Finish	22,340.
KFM-600S	5' 9"	"Millennium" Poished Ivory/White	21,740.
SKG-650S	6' 1"	Ebony	14,940.
SKG-650S	6' 1"	Polished Ebony	14,340.
SKG-650S	6' 1"	Satin/Polished Wood Finishes	14,940.

*For explanation of terms and prices, please see pages 42–48.

Kohler & Campbell (continued)

Model	Size	Style and Finish	Price*
SKG-650S	6' 1"	Polished Ivory/White	14,940.
SKG-650SL	6' 1"	Empire Ebony	15,940.
SKG-650SL	6' 1"	Empire Polished Ebony	15,340.
SKG-650SL	6' 1"	Empire Satin/Polished Wood Finishes	15,940.
SKG-650SL	6' 1"	Empire Polished Ivory/White	15,940.
KFM-650S	6' 1"	"Millennium" Ebony	23,740.
KFM-650S	6' 1"	"Millennium" Polished Ebony	23,340.
KFM-650S	6' 1"	"Millennium" Semi-Gloss Wood Finish	24,340.
KFM-650S	6' 1"	"Millennium" Polished Ivory/White	23,740.
KFM-650SL	6' 1"	"Millennium" Empire Ebony	24,740.
KFM-650SL	6' 1"	"Millennium" Empire Polished Ebony	24,340.
KFM-650SL	6' 1"	"Millennium" Empire Semi-Gloss Wood Finish	25,340.
KFM-650SL	6' 1"	"Millennium" Empire Pol. Ivory/White	24,740.
KFM-700S	6' 8"	"Millennium" Ebony	25,740.
KFM-700S	6' 8"	"Millennium" Polished Ebony	25,340.
KFM-700S	6' 8"	"Millennium" Semi-Gloss Wood Finish	26,340.
KFM-700S	6' 8"	"Millennium" Polished Ivory/White	25,740.
KFM-800S	7'	"Millennium" Polished Ebony	26,250.
KFM-850S	7' 4"	"Millennium" Polished Ebony	28,250.
KFM-900S	9' 1"	"Millennium" Polished Ebony	68,340.

Krakauer

Verticals

Model	Size	Style and Finish	Price*
K443	44"	French Cherry	3,190.
K444	44"	French Oak	3,190.
K445	44"	Oak	3,190.
K446	44"	Cherry	3,190.
K110B	44"	Polished Ebony	3,190.
K110R	44"	Polished Mahogany	3,190.
K110T	44"	Polished Walnut	3,190.
K110W	44"	Polished White	3,190.
K120B	48"	Polished Ebony	3,390.
K120R	48"	Polished Mahogany	3,390.
K120T	48"	Polished Walnut	3,390.

Model	Size	Style and Finish	Price*
K120W	48"	Polished White	3,390.
K122	48-3/4"	*Polished Ebony*	3,500.
K122	48-3/4"	*Polished Mahogany*	3,500.
K122	48-3/4"	*Polished Walnut*	3,500.
K122	48-3/4"	*Polished White*	3,500.
K125	50"	*Polished Ebony*	3,590.
K125	50"	*Polished Mahogany*	3,590.
K125	50"	*Polished Walnut*	3,590.
K125	50"	*Polished White*	3,590.
Grands			
KG-155	5' 1"	Polished Ebony	7,590.

Mason & Hamlin

Verticals			
50	50"	Polished Ebony	17,012.
Grands			
A	5' 8"	Ebony	43,208.
A	5' 8"	Polished Ebony	46,206.
A	5' 8"	Mahogany	46,458.
A	5' 8"	Polished Pyramid Mahogany	56,474.
A	5' 8"	Rosewood	51,566.
A	5' 8"	Bubinga	51,566.
A	5' 8"	Polished Bubinga	54,564.
A	5' 8"	"Monticello" Polished Ebony	49,220.
A	5' 8"	"Monticello" Mahogany	49,458.
A	5' 8"	"Monticello" Rosewood	59,956.
BB	7'	Ebony	56,498.
BB	7'	Polished Ebony	58,122.
BB	7'	Mahogany	58,498.
BB	7'	Polished Pyramid Mahogany	69,648.
BB	7'	Rosewood	65,484.
BB	7'	Bubinga	65,484.
BB	7'	Polished Bubinga	67,108.
BB	7'	"Monticello" Polished Ebony	60,898.
BB	7'	"Monticello" Mahogany	61,498.
BB	7'	"Monticello" Rosewood	75,472.

*For explanation of terms and prices, please see pages 42–48.

Miller, Henry F.

Verticals

Model	Size	Style and Finish	Price
HMV-043	42-1/2"	Continental Polished Ebony	2,998.
HMV-043	42-1/2"	Continental Polished Mahogany	3,092.
HMV-045	43-1/2"	Italian Provincial Cherry	3,656.
HMV-045	43-1/2"	French Provincial Cherry	3,656.
HMV-045	43-1/2"	Mediterranean Oak	3,656.
HMV-047	46-1/2"	Polished Ebony	3,938.
HMV-047	46-1/2"	Polished Mahogany	4,032.

Grands

Model	Size	Style and Finish	Price
HMG-056	4' 8"	Polished Ebony	7,792.
HMG-056	4' 8"	Polished Mahogany	8,074.
HMG-063	5' 3"	Polished Ebony	9,390.
HMG-063	5' 3"	Polished Mahogany	9,872.

Niendorf

Prices do not include bench. Although prices include estimated duty and shipping, because dealers purchase directly from the manufacturer, actual price at time of sale may vary depending on the value of the Euro, the dealer's location, and the shipping method utilized. The prices here were calculated at Euro=$1.11.

Grands

Model	Size	Style and Finish	Price
145	4' 9"	Polished Ebony	26,378.
145	4' 9"	Polished Dark Mahogany	26,378.
145	4' 9"	Polished Medium Walnut	26,378.
145	4' 9"	Chippendale Polished Ebony	27,263.
145	4' 9"	Chippendale Polished Dark Mahogany	27,263.
145	4' 9"	Chippendale Polished Medium Walnut	27,263.
182	6'	Polished Ebony	30,690.
182	6'	Polished Dark Mahogany	30,690.
182	6'	Polished Medium Walnut	30,690.

Nordiska

Verticals

Model	Size	Style and Finish	Price*
109-CM	43"	Continental Polished Ebony	2,480.
109-CM	43"	Continental Polished Mahogany	2,480.
112-F	44"	Continental Polished Ebony	2,780.
112-F	44"	Continental Polished Dark Walnut	2,780.
112-F	44"	Continental Polished Mahogany	2,780.
114-MC	45"	French Walnut	3,580.
114-MC	45"	French Mahogany	3,580.
114-MCH	45"	Continental Walnut	3,580.
114-MCH	45"	Continental Mahogany	3,580.
116-C	46"	Polished Ebony	3,180.
116-C	46"	Polished Dark Walnut	3,180.
116-C	46"	Polished Mahogany	3,180.
116-CB	46"	Chippendale Polished Ebony	3,580.
116-CB	46"	Chippendale Polished Dark Walnut	3,580.
116-CB	46"	Chippendale Polished Mahogany	3,580.
120-C	47"	Polished Ebony	3,780.
120-C	47"	Walnut	3,780.
120-GS	47"	Demi-Chippendale Polished Ebony	3,380.
120-GS	47"	Demi-Chippendale Polished Mahogany	3,380.
118-C GT	48"	Polished Ebony	3,380.
118-MC	48"	Walnut	3,780.
118-MC	48"	Mahogany	3,780.
120-CA	48"	Chippendale Polished Ebony	3,780.
120-CA	48"	Chippendale Polished Mahogany	3,780.
122-C	48"	Polished Ebony	3,780.
122-C	48"	Polished Mahogany	3,780.
126-Pro	50"	Polished Ebony	4,980.
126-Pro	50"	Polished Walnut	4,980.

Grands

Model	Size	Style and Finish	Price*
152-C	5'	Polished Ebony	7,980.
152-C	5'	Polished Mahogany	8,380.
152-C	5'	Sapeli and Polished Sapeli	8,380.
152-C	5'	Polished Walnut	8,380.
152-C	5'	Polished Cherry	8,380.

*For explanation of terms and prices, please see pages 42–48.

Model	Size	Style and Finish	Price*

Nordiska (continued)

Model	Size	Style and Finish	Price*
152-C	5'	Polished White	8,380.
152-DC	5'	Demi-Chippendale Polished Ebony	8,900.
152-DC	5'	Demi-Chippendale Polished Mahogany	9,180.
152-DC	5'	Demi-Chippendale Pol. Dark Walnut	9,180.
152-DC	5'	Demi-Chippendale Polished Sapeli	9,180.
165-CM	5' 5"	Polished Ebony	9,180.
165-CM	5' 5"	Polished Mahogany	9,500.
165-CM	5' 5"	Polished Dark Walnut	9,500.
165-CM	5' 5"	Sapeli and Polished Sapeli	9,500.
165-DC	5' 5"	Demi-Chippendale Polished Ebony	10,180.
165-DC	5' 5"	Demi-Chippendale Polished Mahogany	10,500.
165-DC	5' 5"	Demi-Chippendale Pol. Dark Walnut	10,500.
165-PL	5' 5"	Polished Cherry	9,900.
165-R	5' 5"	Regency Polished Ebony	9,780.
165-R	5' 5"	Regency Polished Mahogany	10,100.
185-C	6' 1"	Polished Ebony	10,980.
185-C	6' 1"	Polished Mahogany	11,300.
185-C	6' 1"	Polished Dark Walnut	11,300.
185-I	6' 1"	Imperial Polished Ebony	11,580.
185-I	6' 1"	Imperial Polished Mahogany	11,900.
185-PN	6' 1"	Polished Ebony	11,380.
215-C	7'	Polished Ebony	19,580.

Pearl River

Verticals

Model	Size	Style and Finish	Price*
UP-108D1	42-1/2"	Continental Polished Ebony	2,750.
UP-108D1	42-1/2"	Continental Polished Mahogany	2,802.
UP-108D1	42-1/2"	Continental Polished Light Walnut	2,802.
UP-108D2	42-1/2"	Continental Polished Cherry	2,802.
UP-108D1	42-1/2"	Continental Polished White	2,854.
UP-108M2	42-1/2"	Chippendale Polished Ebony	2,884.
UP-108M2	42-1/2"	Chippendale Polished Mahogany	2,936.
UP-108M2	42-1/2"	Chippendale Polished Light Walnut	2,936.
UP-108M2	42-1/2"	Chippendale Polished White	2,976.

Model	Size	Style and Finish	Price*
UP-108T2	42-1/2"	Euro-Studio Polished Ebony	2,988.
UP-108T2	42-1/2"	Euro-Studio Polished Mahogany	3,038.
UP-108T2	42-1/2"	Euro-Studio Polished Light Walnut	3,038.
UP-108T2	42-1/2"	Euro-Studio Polished White	3,080.
UP-110P1	43"	Walnut (Boston fallboard)	3,460.
UP-110P1	43"	Cherry (Boston fallboard)	3,460.
UP-110P1	43"	Oak (Boston fallboard)	3,564.
UP-110P2	43"	Country French Oak	3,666.
UP-110P2	43"	Country French Cherry	3,564.
UP-110P2	43"	Country French Maple	3,564.
UP-110P3	43"	"Amerasian" Ebony	3,646.
UP-110P3	43"	"Amerasian" Mahogany	3,698.
UP-110P5	43"	Walnut (Boston fallboard)	3,564.
UP-110P5	43"	Cherry (Boston fallboard)	3,564.
UP-115M1	45"	Polished Ebony (school)	3,018.
UP-115M1	45"	Polished Mahogany (school)	3,060.
UP-115M1	45"	Polished Walnut (school)	3,060.
UP-115P	45"	American Walnut	3,894.
UP-115P	45"	Cherry	3,894.
UP-118M	46-1/2"	Polished Ebony	3,152.
UP-118M	46-1/2"	Polished Mahogany	3,204.
UP-118M	46-1/2"	Polished Walnut	3,204.
UP-118M	46-1/2"	Polished Cherry	3,204.
UP-118M	46-1/2"	Polished White	3,244.
UP-118M4	46-1/2"	Polished Ebony	3,286.
UP-118M4	46-1/2"	Polished Mahogany	3,338.
UP-118M4	46-1/2"	Polished Walnut	3,338.
UP-125M1	49"	Polished Ebony (with Yamaha)	4,614.
UP-130T2	51"	Euro-Design Polished Ebony	5,120.
UP-130T2	51"	Euro-Design Polished Mahogany	5,170.
Grands			
GP-142	4' 7"	Polished Ebony	8,384.
GP-142	4' 7"	Polished Mahogany	8,724.
GP-142	4' 7"	Polished Walnut	8,724.
GP-142	4' 7"	Polished White	8,724.
GP-159	5' 3"	Polished Ebony	10,136.
GP-159	5' 3"	Polished Mahogany	10,476.

*For explanation of terms and prices, please see pages 42–48.

Model	Size	Style and Finish	Price*

Pearl River (continued)

Model	Size	Style and Finish	Price*
GP-159	5' 3"	Polished Walnut	10,476.
GP-159	5' 3"	Polished White	10,476.
GP-183	6'	Polished Ebony	14,142.
GP-183	6'	Polished Mahogany	14,472.
GP-183	6'	Polished Walnut	14,472.
GP-183	6'	Polished White	14,472.
GP-188	6' 4"	Polished Ebony	16,680.
GP-188	6' 4"	Polished Mahogany	17,800.
GP-188	6' 4"	Polished Walnut	17,800.
GP-188	6' 4"	Polished White	17,800.
GP-213	7'	Polished Ebony	18,520.
GP-213	7'	Polished Walnut	18,830.
GP-213	7'	Polished White	18,830.
GP-275	9'	Polished Ebony	on request
GP-275	9'	Polished Walnut	on request
GP-275	9'	Polished White	on request

Perzina, Gebr.

Verticals

Model	Size	Style and Finish	Price*
GD-118AB	47"	Continental Polished Ebony	5,990.
GD-121BB	48"	Polished Ebony	6,890.
GD-121BC	48"	Polished Mahogany	7,190.
GD-121BC	48"	Polished Walnut	7,190.
GD-121C	48"	Ebony with Mahogany Center	7,190.
GS-128BB	51"	Polished Ebony	7,490.
GS-128BC	51"	Polished Mahogany	7,990.
GS-128BC	51"	Polished Walnut	7,990.

Grands

Model	Size	Style and Finish	Price*
P-160BB	5' 2"	Polished Ebony	16,090.
P-160BC	5' 2"	Polished Mahogany	16,690.
P-160BC	5' 2"	Polished Walnut	16,690.
P-160BC	5' 2"	Polished Ivory	16,690.
P-160BC	5' 2"	Polished White	16,690.
E-160BB	5' 2"	Polished Ebony	18,890.

Model	Size	Style and Finish	Price*
E-160BC	5' 2"	Polished Mahogany	19,490.
E-160BC	5' 2"	Polished Walnut	19,490.
E-160BC	5' 2"	Polished Ivory	19,490.
E-160BC	5' 2"	Polished White	19,490.
P-187BB	6' 1"	Polished Ebony	18,190.
P-187BC	6' 1"	Polished Mahogany	19,090.
P-187BC	6' 1"	Polished Walnut	19,090.
P-187BC	6' 1"	Polished Ivory	19,090.
P-187BC	6' 1"	Polished White	19,090.
E-187BB	6' 1"	Polished Ebony	20,990.
E-187BC	6' 1"	Polished Mahogany	21,890.
E-187BC	6' 1"	Polished Walnut	21,890.
E-187BC	6' 1"	Polished Ivory	21,890.
E-187BC	6' 1"	Polished White	21,890.

Petrof

Note: Prices below do not include bench. Add from $220 to $630 (most are under $400), depending on choice of bench.

Verticals

Model	Size	Style and Finish	Price
100-B	42"	"Barok" Polished Walnut	7,100.
100-B	42"	"Barok" Polished Flame Mahogany	7,100.
105-V	43"	Contemporary Polished Walnut	5,380.
105-V	43"	Contemporary Polished Mahogany	5,380.
115-I	45"	Demi-Chippendale Polished Ebony	6,700.
115-I	45"	Demi-Chipp. Pol. Walnut w/Designer Panel	6,900.
115-I	45"	Demi-Chipp. Pol. Mahog. w/Designer Panel	6,900.
115-IC	45"	Chippendale Polished Ebony	6,980.
115-IC	45"	Chippendale Polished Walnut	6,980.
115-IC	45"	Chippendale Polished Flame Mahogany	6,980.
115-II	45"	Continental Polished Ebony	5,980.
115-II	45"	Continental Polished Walnut	5,980.
115-IID P/R	45"	Polished Ebony	6,780.
115-IID P/R	45"	Polished Walnut	6,780.
115-IID P/R	45"	Polished Flame Mahogany	6,780.
115-V	45"	Polished Ebony	6,580.
115-V	45"	Polished Walnut	6,580.

*For explanation of terms and prices, please see pages 42–48.

Model	Size	Style and Finish	Price*

Petrof (continued)

Model	Size	Style and Finish	Price*
115-V	45"	Polished Flame Mahogany	6,580.
115-VI	45"	Polished Walnut	6,380.
115-VI	45"	Polished Walnut with Marquetry	6,580.
115-VI	45"	Polished Walnut w/Designer Panel	6,500.
115-VI	45"	Polished Mahogany	6,380.
115-VI	45"	Polished Mahogany with Marquetry	6,580.
115-VI	45"	Polished Mahogany w/Designer Panel	6,500.
115-VI	45"	"Elegance" Polished Ebony w/Brass	6,180.
115-VII	45"	Polished Alpi Walnut Veneer	6,580.
125-III	50"	Polished Walnut	7,700.
125-III	50"	Polished Walnut with Fan Design	7,900.
125-III	50"	Polished Walnut w/Designer Panel	7,780.
125-III	50"	Polished Mahogany	7,700.
125-III	50"	Polished Mahogany with Fan Design	7,900.
125-III	50"	Polished Mahogany w/Designer Panel	7,780.
125-IV	50"	Polished Ebony	7,780.
126-III	50"	"Elegante" Pol. Ebony w/Walnut/Brass	8,300.
131	52"	Polished Ebony	10,500.
131	52"	Polished Walnut	10,500.
131	52"	Polished Flame Mahogany	10,500.
135	53"	"Klasik" Polished Ebony	14,500.

Grands

Model	Size	Style and Finish	Price*
V	5' 3"	Polished Ebony	19,980.
V	5' 3"	Polished Walnut	19,980.
V	5' 3"	Polished Flame Mahogany	19,980.
V	5' 3"	Polished White	20,780.
V DC	5' 3"	Demi-Chippendale Polished Ebony	22,400.
V DC	5' 3"	Demi-Chippendale Polished Walnut	22,400.
V DC	5' 3"	Demi-Chippendale Pol. Flame Mahog.	22,400.
IV	5' 8"	Polished Ebony	21,600.
IV	5' 8"	Polished Walnut	21,600.
IV	5' 8"	Polished Flame Mahogany	21,600.
IV	5' 8"	Polished White	21,800.
IV DC	5' 8"	Demi-Chippendale Polished Ebony	23,600.
IV DC	5' 8"	Demi-Chippendale Polished Walnut	23,600.

Model	Size	Style and Finish	Price*
IV DC	5' 8"	Demi-Chippendale Pol. Flame Mahog.	23,600.
IV Klasik	5' 8"	Demi-Chippendale Polished Ebony	25,600.
IV Klasik	5' 8"	Demi-Chippendale Polished Walnut	25,600.
IV Klasik	5' 8"	Demi-Chippendale Pol. Flame Mahog.	25,600.
III	6' 4"	Polished Ebony	25,800.
III	6' 4"	Polished Walnut	25,800.
III	6' 4"	Polished Flame Mahogany	25,800.
III Majestic	6' 4"	Polished Ebony	27,800.
III Majestic	6' 4"	Polished Walnut	27,800.
III Majestic	6' 4"	Polished Flame Mahogany	27,800.
II	7' 9"	"Symphony" Polished Ebony	39,000.
II	7' 9"	"Symphony" Polished Walnut	39,000.
I	9' 3"	"Mondial" Polished Ebony	49,000.
P1	9' 3"	*"Mistral" Polished Ebony*	69,000.

PianoDisc

Prices for PianoDisc and QuietTime systems vary by piano manufacturer and installer. The following are suggested retail prices from PianoDisc. The usual dealer discounts may apply, especially as an incentive to purchase a piano.

228 CFX System, "factory-installed" or retrofitted:

Playback only	6,489.
Add for SymphonyPro Sound Module	1,429.
Add for TFT MIDI Record system	1,429.
Add for amplified speakers, pair	824.
Add for MX (Music Expansion) Basic	1,429.
Add for MX (Music Expansion) Platinum	1,869.
Add for PianoAmp	505.
Add for PianoMute Rail	439.
Add for Home Theater Master Remote	499.

PianoCD System	5,499.
QuietTime GT System (TFT MIDI Strip, MIDI interface board, pedal switches, cable, headphones, power supply, PianoMute rail)	2,188.
MIDI Controller (TFT MIDI Strip, MIDI interface board, pedal switches, cable, power supply)	2,034.

*For explanation of terms and prices, please see pages 42–48.

Pleyel

Verticals

Model	Size	Style and Finish	Price*
Esprit	45"	Polished Ebony	8,900.
Academie	45"	Polished Ebony	9,400.
Academie	45"	Walnut	9,800.
Academie	45"	Polished White	9,800.
P 118	47"	Polished Ebony	10,300.
P 118	47"	Polished Mahogany	12,100.
P 118	47"	*Walnut with Marquetry*	11,400.
P 118	47"	Cherry with Marquetry	11,400.
P 118	47"	"Romantica Noyer" Walnut	11,200.
P 124	49"	Polished Ebony	11,600.
P 124	49"	*Walnut with Marquetry*	13,000.
P 124	49"	Cherry with Marquetry	13,000.
P 131	51"	Polished Ebony	15,000.
P 131	51"	Polished Mahogany	15,900.
P 131	51"	*With Sostenuto, add*	700.

Grands

Model	Size	Style and Finish	Price*
P 170	5' 7"	Polished Ebony	35,400.
P 170	5' 7"	Polished Mahogany	43,000.
P 170	5' 7"	Walnut	39,200.
P 190	6' 3"	Polished Ebony	43,000.
P 190	6' 3"	Cherry with Marquetry	50,700.
P 190	6' 3"	Polished Mahogany	50,700.

Pramberger

Verticals

Model	Size	Style and Finish	Price*
JP-48	48"	Polished Ebony	7,390.
JP-48	48"	Brown Mahogany	7,990.
JP-48	48"	Bubinga	7,990.
JP-48	48"	Rosewood	7,990.
JP-48	48"	Cherry	7,990.
JP-48	48"	Apple	7,990.
JP-52	52"	Polished Ebony	9,390.
JP-52	52"	Bubinga	9,990.
JP-52	52"	Rosewood	9,990.

Model	Size	Style and Finish	Price*
Grands			
JP-175	5' 9"	Polished Ebony	17,390.
JP-175	5' 9"	Polished Ebony with Pommele Inlay	18,190.
JP-175	5' 9"	Polished Red Mahogany	18,990.
JP-175	5' 9"	Polished Brown Mahogany	18,990.
JP-175	5' 9"	Polished Kewazinga Bubinga	20,590.
JP-185	6' 1"	Polished Ebony	21,990.
JP-185	6' 1"	Polished Ebony with Pommele Inlay	22,990.
JP-185	6' 1"	Polished Red Mahogany	23,990.
JP-185	6' 1"	Polished Brown Mahogany	23,990.
JP-185	6' 1"	Polished Kewazinga Bubinga	25,990.
JP-185	6' 1"	Polished Santos Rosewood	27,990.
JP-185	6' 1"	Polished African Pommele	28,990.
JP-208	6' 10"	Polished Ebony	25,990.
JP-208	6' 10"	Polished Ebony with Pommele Inlay	27,190.
JP-208	6' 10"	Polished Kewazinga Bubinga	30,990.
JP-208	6' 10"	Polished Santos Rosewood	32,990.
JP-208	6' 10"	Polished Birch Burl	33,990.
JP-208	6' 10"	Polished African Pommele	34,500.
JP-228	7' 6"	Polished Ebony	36,380.
JP-228	7' 6"	Polished Kewazinga Bubinga	40,580.
JP-228	7' 6"	Polished Santos Rosewood	41,980.
JP-228	7' 6"	Polished African Pommele	42,780.

QRS / Pianomation

Prices for Pianomation systems vary by piano manufacturer, installer, and accessories. The following are approximate retail prices for installed systems from QRS. The usual dealer discounts may apply, especially as an incentive to purchase a piano.

Pianomation:	2000C Player System	5,220.
	2000CD+ Player System, CD player, speaker	5,975.
	Chili System with CD and floppy drives, record strip, speaker	9,000.
	Serenade CD with CD drive, speaker	6,375.
	Serenade Pro with CD, floppy, and hard drives, record strip, speaker	10,100.

*For explanation of terms and prices, please see pages 42–48.

Model	Size	Style and Finish	Price*

QRS / Pianomation (continued)

Playola:		With 2000C Player System	6,000.
		With 2000CD+ Player System	6,750.
Practice Session with record strip, piano-only sound, stop rail			950.

Ridgewood

Verticals

Model	Size	Style and Finish	Price
AV-110	44"	French Provincial Cherry	3,450.
AV-110	44"	Queen Anne Maple	3,450.
AV-112	44-1/2"	Continental Polished Ebony	2,910.
AV-112	44-1/2"	Continental Polished Mahogany	2,990.

Grands

Model	Size	Style and Finish	Price
AG-152	5'	Polished Ebony	8,590.
AG-152	5'	Polished Mahogany	8,910.
AG-152	5'	Polished Walnut	8,910.
AG-152D	5'	Queen Anne Polished Mahogany	9,540.
AG-152D	5'	Louis XIV Polished Ebony	9,540.
AG-165	5' 5"	Polished Ebony	10,390.

Ritmüller

Verticals

Model	Size	Style and Finish	Price
UP-110R2	43-1/2"	"Elegant" Continental Polished Ebony	3,182.
UP-110R2	43-1/2"	"Elegant" Continental Pol. Mahogany	3,234.
UP-110R2	43-1/2"	"Elegant" Continental Polished Walnut	3,234.
UP-110R2	43-1/2"	"Elegant" Continental Polished White	3,234.
UP-118R1	46-1/2"	"Designer" Polished Ebony	3,688.
UP-118R1	46-1/2"	"Designer" Polished Mahogany	3,750.
UP-118R1	46-1/2"	"Designer" Polished Walnut	3,750.
UP-118R2	46-1/2"	"Scandinavian Design" Polished Ebony	3,522.
UP-118R2	46-1/2"	"Scandinavian Design" Pol. Mahogany	4,018.
UP-118R2	46-1/2"	"Scandinavian Design" Pol. Catalpa	4,018.
UP-120R	48"	Polished Ebony	4,038.
UP-120R	48"	Polished Mahogany	4,100.
UP-120R	48"	Polished Walnut	4,100.

Model	Size	Style and Finish	Price*
UP-120R1	48"	"European Designer" Pol. Ebony w/Mahog.	4,162.
UP-120R1	48"	"European Designer" Pol. Emerald w/Oak	4,212.
UP-120R2	48"	Chippendale Walnut	4,522.
UP-120R2	48"	Chippendale Cherry	4,522.
UP-120R3	48"	"Euro Modern" Cherry	4,512.
UP-123R	48"	"Classic Euro" Mahogany	4,964.
UP-123R	48"	"Classic Euro" Polished Mahogany	4,964.
UP-123R	48"	"Classic Euro" Polished Walnut	4,964.
UP-125R	49"	"New-European" Polished Ebony	5,438.
UP-126R	50"	"Designer Classic" Pol. Eb. w/Burl Walnut	5,326.
UP-130R	51"	Ebony	5,562.
UP-130R	51"	Walnut	5,624.
Grands			
GP-142R	4' 7"	Polished Ebony	8,888.
GP-142R	4' 7"	Polished Mahogany	9,250.
GP-142R	4' 7"	Polished Walnut	9,250.
GP-142R	4' 7"	Polished White	9,250.
GP-142R1	4' 7"	Ebony and Polished Ebony	8,786.
GP-142R1	4' 7"	Polished Mahogany	9,146.
GP-142R1	4' 7"	Polished Walnut	9,146.
GP-142R1	4' 7"	Polished White	9,146.
GP-159R	5' 3"	Polished Ebony	11,906.
GP-159R	5' 3"	Polished Mahogany	12,236.
GP-159R	5' 3"	Polished Walnut	12,236.
GP-159R	5' 3"	Polished White	12,236.
GP-159R1	5' 3"	"Euro-Modern" Polished Ebony	11,700.
GP-159R1	5' 3"	"Euro-Modern" Polished Mahogany	12,030.
GP-159R1	5' 3"	"Euro-Modern" Polished Walnut	12,030.
GP-183R	6'	Polished Ebony	14,874.
GP-183R	6'	Polished Mahogany	15,202.
GP-183R1	6'	Ebony and Polished Ebony	14,770.
GP-183R1	6'	Polished Mahogany	15,100.
GP-213R1	7'	Polished Ebony	19,026.
GP-213R1	7'	Polished Mahogany	19,394.
GP-213R1	7'	Polished Walnut	19,394.
GP-213R1	7'	Polished White	19,394.

*For explanation of terms and prices, please see pages 42–48.

Samick

In general, "Wood Finishes" means mahogany, walnut, cherry, and brown oak. However, even where not specifically indicated, most models are available by special order in any finish.

Verticals

Model	Size	Style and Finish	Price
JS-042	42"	Continental Ebony	3,140.
JS-042	42"	Continental Polished Ebony	3,040.
JS-042	42"	Continental Satin/Pol. Wood Finishes	3,140.
JS-042	42"	Continental Polished Ivory/White	3,140.
JS-143F	44"	French Provincial Wood Finishes	3,840.
JS-143M	44"	Mediterranean Wood Finishes	3,740.
JS-143T	44"	Wood Finishes	3,840.
JS-115	45"	Ebony	3,340.
JS-115	45"	Polished Ebony	3,240.
JS-115	45"	Satin/Polished Wood Finishes	3,340.
JS-115	45"	Polished Ivory/White	3,340.
JS-118F	46-1/2"	French Provincial Wood Finishes	4,440.
JS-118M	46-1/2"	Mediterranean Wood Finishes	4,240.
JS-118T	46-1/2"	Wood Finishes	4,440.
JS-247	46-1/2"	Ebony and Polished Ebony	4,940.
JS-247	46-1/2"	Satin and Polished Wood Finishes	4,940.
JS-121F	48"	French Provincial Ebony	4,540.
JS-121F	48"	French Provincial Polished Ebony	4,340.
JS-121F	48"	French Prov. Satin/Pol. Wood Finishes	4,540.
JS-121M	48"	Mediterranean Ebony	4,540.
JS-121M	48"	Mediterranean Polished Ebony	4,260.
JS-121M	48"	Mediterranean Satin/Pol. Wood Finishes	4,540.

Grands

Model	Size	Style and Finish	Price
SIG-50	4' 11-1/2"	Ebony	8,940.
SIG-50	4' 11-1/2"	Polished Ebony	8,340.
SIG-50	4' 11-1/2"	Polished Mahogany	8,940.
SIG-50	4' 11-1/2"	Polished Walnut	8,940.
SIG-50	4' 11-1/2"	Polished Ivory/White	8,940.
SIG-54	5' 3"	Ebony	10,340.
SIG-54	5' 3"	Polished Ebony	9,940.
SIG-54	5' 3"	Polished Mahogany	10,340.
SIG-54	5' 3"	Polished Walnut	10,340.

Model	Size	Style and Finish	Price*
SIG-54	5' 3"	Polished Ivory/White	10,340.
SG-172	5' 7"	Ebony	14,140.
SG-172	5' 7"	Polished Ebony	13,540.
SG-172	5' 7"	Satin and Polished Wood Finishes	14,140.
SG-172	5' 7"	Polished Ivory/White	14,140.
SG-172L	5' 7"	Empire Ebony	15,140.
SG-172L	5' 7"	Emprie Polished Ebony	14,540.
SG-172L	5' 7"	Empire Satin/Polished Wood Finishes	15,140.
SG-172L	5' 7"	Empire Polished Ivory/White	15,140.
SG-185	6' 1"	Ebony	14,940.
SG-185	6' 1"	Polished Ebony	14,340.
SG-185	6' 1"	Satin and Polished Wood Finishes	14,940.
SG-185	6' 1"	Polished Ivory/White	14,940.
SG-185L	6' 1"	Empire Ebony	15,940.
SG-185L	6' 1"	Empire Polished Ebony	15,340.
SG-185L	6' 1"	Empire Satin and Pol. Wood Finishes	15,940.
SG-185L	6' 1"	Empire Polished Ivory/White	15,940.

Sängler & Söhne / Wieler

Verticals

C43R	43"	Oak (round leg)	2,990.
C43R	43"	Mahogany (round leg)	2,900.
C43F	43"	French Oak	2,990.
C43F	43"	French Mahogany	2,990.
111GD	44"	Continental Polished Ebony	2,500.
111GD	44"	Continental Polished Mahogany	2,550.
111GD	44"	Continental Polished Walnut	2,550.
111GD	44"	Continental Polished White	2,550.
115GC	45"	Chippendale Polished Ebony	2,750.
115GC	45"	Chippendale Polished Mahogany	2,790.
450	45"	Italian Provincial Walnut	3,190.
450	45"	Italian Provincial Mahogany	3,190.
450	45"	Italian Provincial Cherry	3,190.
451	45"	Walnut (round leg)	3,190.
451	45"	Mahogany (round leg)	3,190.
451	45"	Cherry (round leg)	3,190.
452	45"	French Walnut	3,190.

*For explanation of terms and prices, please see pages 42–48.

Model	Size	Style and Finish	Price*

Sängler & Söhne / Wieler (continued)

Model	Size	Style and Finish	Price*
452	45"	French Mahogany	3,190.
452	45"	French Cherry	3,190.
115WH	46"	Polished Ebony	2,790.
115WH	46"	Polished Mahogany	2,840.
115WH	46"	Polished Walnut	2,840.
121WH	48"	Polished Ebony	3,100.
121WH	48"	Polished Mahogany	3,100.
121WH	48"	Polished Walnut	3,100.
131X	52"	Polished Ebony	3,990.
131X	52"	Polished Mahogany	4,190.
Grands			
450	4' 7"	Polished Ebony	8,500.
450	4' 7"	Polished Mahogany	8,840.
450	4' 7"	Polished Brown Oak	8,840.
148SR	4' 11"	Victorian Polished Ebony	8,990.
148SR	4' 11"	Victorian Polished Mahogany	8,990.
148SR	4' 11"	Victorian Polished Walnut	8,990.
152DP	5'	Polished Ebony	7,990.
152DP	5'	Polished Mahogany	8,390.
152DP	5'	Polished Walnut	8,390.
152DP	5'	Polished White	8,390.
480	5' 1"	Polished Ebony	9,770.
480	5' 1"	Polished Mahogany	10,110.
165DP	5' 4"	Polished Ebony	8,590.
165DP	5' 4"	Polished Mahogany	9,190.
165DP	5' 4"	Polished Walnut	9,190.
165DP	5' 4"	Polished White	9,190.
185DP	6' 1"	Polished Ebony	9,990.
185DP	6' 1"	Polished Mahogany	10,390.

Sauter

Verticals			
122	48"	"Competence" Polished Ebony	21,840.
122	48"	"Domino" Polished Ebony	17,510.

Model	Size	Style and Finish	Price*
122	48"	"Domino" Pear	17,510.
122	48"	"Resonance" Cherry/Yew	21,750.
122	48"	"Schulpiano" Beech	14,880.
122	48"	"Vista" Polished Ebony	18,930.
122	48"	"Vista" Maple	17,960.
122	48"	"Vista" Pear	19,720.
122	48"	"Vista" Cherry	19,190.
122	48"	"M-Line M2" Polished Ebony	23,050.
128	50"	"M-Line M1" Polished Ebony	26,960.

Grands

Model	Size	Style and Finish	Price*
160	5' 3"	"Alpha" Polished Ebony	46,200.
160	5' 3"	"Alpha" Walnut	41,890.
160	5' 3"	"Alpha" Mahogany	41,890.
160	5' 3"	"Alpha" Polished White	47,680.
160	5' 3"	Chippendale Walnut	45,640.
160	5' 3"	Chippendale Mahogany	45,640.
160	5' 3"	Chippendale Cherry	51,720.
160	5' 3"	"Noblesse" Walnut	47,190.
160	5' 3"	"Noblesse" Mahogany	47,190.
160	5' 3"	"Noblesse" Cherry	50,830.
185	6' 1"	"Delta" Polished Ebony	50,440.
185	6' 1"	"Delta" Walnut	46,220.
185	6' 1"	"Delta" Mahogany	46,220.
185	6' 1"	Chippendale Walnut	51,500.
185	6' 1"	Chippendale Mahogany	51,500.
185	6' 1"	Chippendale Cherry	55,140.
185	6' 1"	"Noblesse" Walnut	53,940.
185	6' 1"	"Noblesse" Mahogany	53,940.
185	6' 1"	"Noblesse" Cherry	55,700.
220	7' 2"	"Omega" Polished Ebony	64,490.
220	7' 2"	"Omega" Walnut	58,400.
220	7' 2"	"Omega" Mahogany	58,400.
275	9'	"Concert" Polished Ebony	109,820.
Satin models		*Additional, for polished finish*	5,400.
Peter Maly models		*Available by special order only*	on request

*For explanation of terms and prices, please see pages 42–48.

Schell, Lothar

Verticals

Model	Size	Style and Finish	Price
LU-110	43"	Polished Ebony	3,100.
LU-110	43"	Polished Walnut	3,200.
LU-110	43"	Polished Mahogany	3,200.
LU-43	43"	Cherry	3,500.
LU-43	43"	Mahogany	3,500.
LU-43F	43"	French Provincial Cherry	3,500.
LU-43F	43"	French Provincial Mahogany	3,500.
LU-115	45"	Polished Ebony	3,400.
LU-115	45"	Polished Walnut	3,500.
LU-115	45"	Polished Mahogany	3,500.
LU-115F	45"	French Provincial Polished Ebony	3,500.
LU-115F	45"	French Provincial Polished Mahogany	3,600.
LU-45	45"	Cherry	3,700.
LU-45	45"	Mahogany	3,700.
LU-45F	45"	French Provincial Cherry	3,700.
LU-45F	45"	French Provincial Mahogany	3,700.
LU-45F	45"	French Provincial Oak	3,700.
LU-120	48"	Polished Ebony	3,700.
LU-120	48"	Polished Walnut	3,800.
LU-120	48"	Polished Mahogany	3,800.

Grands

Model	Size	Style and Finish	Price
LG-152	5'	Polished Ebony	9,300.
LG-152	5'	Polished Mahogany	9,600.
LG-152R	5'	Polished Ebony (round legs)	9,600.
LG-152R	5'	Polished Mahogany (round legs)	9,900.
LG-165	5' 5"	Polished Ebony	10,200.
LG-165	5' 5"	Polished Mahogany	10,500.
LG-165R	5' 5"	Polished Ebony (round legs)	10,600.
LG-165R	5' 5"	Polished Mahogany (round legs)	10,900.
LG-185	6' 1"	Polished Ebony	11,600.
LG-185	6' 1"	Polished Mahogany	11,900.
LG-185R	6' 1"	Polished Ebony (round legs)	12,000.
LG-185R	6' 1"	Polished Mahogany (round legs)	12,300.

Model	Size	Style and Finish	Price*

Schimmel

Verticals

Model	Size	Style and Finish	Price*
116 E	46"	"Exquisite" Polished Ebony	12,780.
116 E	46"	"Exquisite" Polished Mahogany	13,180.
116 E	46"	*"Exquisite" Polished White*	13,180.
116 E	46"	"Exquisite" Alder	13,180.
116 E	46"	"Exquisite" Open-Pore Walnut	13,180.
116 E	46"	"Exquisite" Open-Pore Beech	13,180.
116 E	46"	"Exquisite" Open-Pore Maple	13,180.
116 E	46"	"Exquisite" Open-Pore Ash	13,180.
116 E	46"	"Exquisite" Waxed Plum	13,180.
116 E	46"	"Exquisite" O.P. Waxed Swiss Pear	13,180.
116 S	46"	"Special" Polished Ebony	11,980.
116 S	46"	"Special" Alder	12,780.
116 S	46"	"Special" Open-Pore Walnut	12,780.
116 S	46"	"Special" Open-Pore Birch	12,780.
116 S	46"	"Special" Open-Pore Beech	12,780.
116 S	46"	"Special" Waxed Swiss Pear	12,780.
120 I	48"	"International" Polished Ebony	13,180.
120 I	48"	"International" Polished Mahogany	13,580.
120 I	48"	*"International" Polished White*	13,580.
120 J	48"	"Centennial" Pol. Mahog. with Myrtle Inlay	13,980.
120 J	48"	"Centennial" Pol. Cherry with Yew Inlay	14,380.
120 LE	48"	"Lyra Exquisite" Polished Mahogany	13,580.
120 LE	48"	"Lyra Exquisite" Polished Cherry	13,980.
120 M	48"	"Solid" Open-Pore Waxed Maple	14,980.
120 RI	48"	"Royale Intarsia" Polished Mahogany	15,580.
120 RI	48"	*"Royale Intarsia" Polished Cherry*	15,980.
120 S	48"	"School" Open-Pore Ebony	13,380.
120 TN	48"	"Noblesse" Polished Ebony	13,580.
120 TN	48"	*"Noblesse" Polished White*	13,980.
120 TN-SE	48"	"Noblesse" Sig. Ed. Polished Ebony	13,980.
122 KE	49"	"Classicism Exquisite" Polished Ebony	13,780.
122 KE	49"	"Classicism Exquisite" Pol. Mahogany	14,180.
122 KE	49"	*"Classicism Exquisite" O.P. Waxed Alder*	14,580.
122 KE	49"	*"Classicism Exquisite" Polished Cherry*	14,580.

*For explanation of terms and prices, please see pages 42–48.

Model	Size	Style and Finish	Price*

Schimmel (continued)

Model	Size	Style and Finish	Price*
F 122 AC	49"	"Art Cubus" Polished Ebony	15,500.
F 122 AC	49"	"Art Cubus" Waxed Swiss Pear	15,900.
F 122 SE	49"	"Salon Exquisite" Polished Ebony	14,700.
F 122 SE	49"	"Salon Exquisite" Waxed Swiss Pear	15,100.
S 125 DN	49"	"Diamond Noblesse" Polished Ebony	17,180.
S 125 DN	49"	"Diamond Noblesse" Polished Mahog.	17,580.
S 125 DP	49"	"Diamond Prestige" Polished Ebony	17,580.
S 125 DP	49"	"Diamond Prestige" Pol. Mahogany	17,980.
130 T	51"	Polished Ebony	15,780.
130 T	51"	Polished Mahogany	16,180.
130 T	51"	*Polished Walnut*	16,180.
130 T	51"	*Polished White*	16,180.
130 T-O	51"	Polished Ebony (upper panel oval inlay)	16,180.
O 132 DT	52"	"Diamond Tradition" Polished Ebony	18,200.
O 132 DT	52"	"Diamond Tradition" Pol. Mahogany	18,800.

Grands

When not mentioned, satin finish available on special order at same price as high-polish finish.

Model	Size	Style and Finish	Price*
GP 169 C	5' 7"	Chippendale Polished Mahogany	37,380.
GP 169 C	5' 7"	Chippendale Polished Walnut	37,380.
GP 169 DE	5' 7"	"Diamond Edition" Polished Ebony	36,580.
GP 169 DE	5' 7"	"Diamond Edition" Pol. Pyramid Mahog.	39,980.
GP 169 DE	5' 7"	"Diamond Edition" Polished Bubinga	39,980.
GP 169 DE	5' 7"	"Diamond Edition" Pol. Bird's Eye Maple	39,980.
GP 169 DE	5' 7"	"Diamond Edition" Pol. Swiss Pear	39,980.
GP 169 DE	5' 7"	"Diamond Edition" Macassar	39,980.
GP 169 DE	5' 7"	"Diamond Edition" Polished White	39,980.
GP 169 E	5' 7"	"Empire" Polished Pyramid Mahogany	43,980.
GP 169 T	5' 7"	Polished Ebony	33,980.
GP 169 T	5' 7"	"Hidden Beauty" Pol. Ebony w/Bubinga	36,580.
GP 169 TE	5' 7"	"Exquisite" Polished Ebony	36,380.
GP 169 TE	5' 7"	"Exquisite" Pol. Mahogany	36,980.
GP 169 TE	5' 7"	"Exquisite" Polished White	36,980.
GP 169 TE-I	5' 7"	"Exquisite" Polished Mahogany Intarsia	37,380.
GP 169 TJ	5' 7"	"Jubilee" Polished Ebony	35,980.

Model	Size	Style and Finish	Price*
GP 169 TJ	5' 7"	"Jubilee" Polished Mahogany	36,780.
GP 169 TJ	5' 7"	"Jubilee" Polished Swiss Pear	36,780.
GP 169 TJ	5' 7"	"Jubilee" Polished White	36,780.
SP 182 C	6'	*Chippendale Polished Walnut*	38,980.
SP 182 C	6'	*Chippendale Polished Mahogany*	38,980.
SP 182 DE	6'	"Diamond Edition" Polished Ebony	38,980.
SP 182 DE	6'	"Diamond Edition" Pol. Pyramid Mahog.	42,380.
SP 182 DE	6'	"Diamond Edition" Polished Bubinga	42,380.
SP 182 DE	6'	*"Diamond Edition" Pol. Bird's Eye Maple*	42,380.
SP 182 DE	6'	*"Diamond Edition" Pol. Swiss Pear*	42,380.
SP 182 DE	6'	"Diamond Edition" Macassar	42,380.
SP 182 DE	6'	*"Diamond Edition" Polished White*	42,380.
SP 182 E	6'	Empire Polished Pyramid Mahogany	43,980.
SP 182 S	6'	"School" Open-Pore Oak	34,780.
SP 182 T	6'	Polished Ebony	35,580.
SP 182 T	6'	Polished Walnut	36,380.
SP 182 T	6'	Polished Mahogany	36,380.
SP 182 T	6'	Polished White	36,380.
SP 182 T	6'	"Hidden Beauty" Pol. Ebony w/Bubinga	38,980.
SP 182 TE	6'	"Exquisite" Polished Ebony	37,180.
SP 182 TE	6'	"Exquisite" Polished Mahogany	37,980.
SP 182 TE	6'	*"Exquisite" Polished White*	37,980.
SP 182 TE-I	6'	"Exquisite" Polished Mahogany Intarsia	38,980.
SP 182 TJ	6'	"Jubilee" Polished Ebony	37,580.
SP 182 TJ	6'	"Jubilee" Polished Mahogany	38,380.
SP 182 TJ	6'	*"Jubilee" Polished White*	38,380.
SP 182 TJ	6'	*"Jubilee" Polished Swiss Pear*	38,380.
SP 189 C	6' 3"	*Chippendale Polished Walnut*	41,380.
SP 189 C	6' 3"	*Chippendale Polished Mahogany*	41,380.
SP 189 DE	6' 3"	"Diamond Edition" Polished Ebony	40,580.
SP 189 DE	6' 3"	"Diamond Edition" Pol. Pyramid Mahog.	43,980.
SP 189 DE	6' 3"	"Diamond Edition" Polished Bubinga	43,980.
SP 189 DE	6' 3"	*"Diamond Edition" Pol. Bird's Eye Maple*	43,980.
SP 189 DE	6' 3"	*"Diamond Edition" Pol. Swiss Pear*	43,980.
SP 189 DE	6' 3"	"Diamond Edition" Macassar	43,980.
SP 189 DE	6' 3"	*"Diamond Edition" Polished White*	43,980.
SP 189 E	6' 3"	Empire Polished Pyramid Mahogany	47,980.

*For explanation of terms and prices, please see pages 42–48.

Schimmel (continued)

Model	Size	Style and Finish	Price*
SP 189 S	6' 3"	"School" Open-Pore Oak	36,980.
SP 189 T	6' 3"	Polished Ebony	37,980.
SP 189 T	6' 3"	Polished Walnut	38,780.
SP 189 T	6' 3"	Polished Mahogany	38,780.
SP 189 T	6' 3"	Polished White	38,780.
SP 189 T	6' 3"	"Hidden Beauty" Pol. Ebony w/Bubinga	40,580.
SP 189 TE	6' 3"	"Exquisite" Polished Ebony	40,380.
SP 189 TE	6' 3"	"Exquisite" Polished Mahogany	40,980.
SP 189 TE	6' 3"	"Exquisite" Polished White	40,980.
SP 189 TE-I	6' 3"	"Exquisite" Polished Mahogany Intarsia	41,380.
SP 189 TJ	6' 3"	"Jubilee" Polished Ebony	39,980.
SP 189 TJ	6' 3"	"Jubilee" Polished Mahogany	40,780.
SP 189 TJ	6' 3"	"Jubilee" Polished White	40,780.
SP 189 TJ	6' 3"	"Jubilee" Polished Swiss Pear	40,780.
208 P	7'	*"Pegasus" Acrylic*	179,800.
CC 213 A	7'	*"Art Edition"*	129,800.
CC 213 C	7'	*Chippendale Polished Mahogany*	45,380.
CC 213 C	7'	*Chippendale Polished Walnut*	45,380.
CC 213 DE	7'	"Diamond Edition" Polished Ebony	44,580.
CC 213 DE	7'	*"Diamond Edition" Polished White*	47,980.
CC 213 DE	7'	"Diamond Edition" Pol. Pyramid Mahog.	47,980.
CC 213 DE	7'	"Diamond Edition" Polished Bubinga	47,980.
CC 213 DE	7'	*"Diamond Edition" Pol. Bird's Eye Maple*	47,980.
CC 213 DE	7'	*"Diamond Edition" Pol. Swiss Pear*	47,980.
CC 213 DE	7'	"Diamond Edition" Macassar	47,980.
CC 213 G	7'	*Plexiglass Clear Acrylic*	109,800.
CC 213 S	7'	"School" Open-Pore Oak	40,980.
CC 213 T	7'	Polished Ebony	41,980.
CC 213 T	7'	Polished Mahogany	42,780.
CC 213 T	7'	*Polished White*	42,780.
CC 213 T	7'	*Polished Walnut*	42,780.
CC 213 T	7'	"Hidden Beauty" Pol. Ebony w/Bubinga	44,580.
CC 213 TE	7'	"Exquisite" Polished Ebony	44,380.
CC 213 TE	7'	*"Exquisite" Polished Mahogany*	44,900.
CC 213 TE	7'	*"Exquisite" Polished White*	44,900.

Model	Size	Style and Finish	Price*
CC 213 TJ	7'	"Jubilee" Polished Ebony	43,980.
CC 213 TJ	7'	*"Jubilee" Polished Mahogany*	44,780.
CC 213 TJ	7'	*"Jubilee" Polished White*	44,780.
CC 213 TJ	7'	*"Jubilee" Polished Swiss Pear*	44,780.
CO 256 T	8' 4"	Polished Ebony	66,980.

Schubert

Verticals

B-21	43"	Continental Polished Ebony	2,258.
B-21	43"	Continental Polished Cherry	2,258.
B-21	43"	Continental Polished Oak	2,258.
B-20	44"	Country French Oak	2,440.
B-20	44"	French Provincial Mahogany	2,440.
B-22	44"	Polished Ebony	2,320.
B-22	44"	Polished Mahogany	2,320.
B-22	44"	Polished Oak	2,320.
B-23	44"	Chippendale Polished Ebony	2,440.
B-23	44"	Chippendale Polished Mahogany	2,440.
B-23	44"	Chippendale Polished Walnut	2,440.
B-23	44"	Chippendale Oak	2,440.
B-23	44"	Chippendale Polished Oak	2,440.
B-23	44"	Chippendale Polished Cherry	2,440.
B-7R	47"	Continental Polished Mahogany	1,990.
B-15A	47"	Polished Ebony	2,590.
B-15A	47"	Polished Mahogany	2,590.
B-15A	47"	Polished Walnut	2,590.
B-15A	47"	Polished Oak	2,590.

Schultz & Sons

Model numbers beginning with 3 or 4 designate pianos manufactured by Broadwood, numbers beginning with 7 or 8, by Samick.

Verticals

3807-S	47"	Polished Ebony	19,650.
3807-S	47"	Walnut	18,550.
3807-S	47"	Polished Walnut	20,750.

*For explanation of terms and prices, please see pages 42–48.

Model	Size	Style and Finish	Price*

Schultz & Sons (continued)

Model	Size	Style and Finish	Price*
3807-S	47"	Mahogany	18,550.
3807-S	47"	Polished Mahogany	20,750.
3809-S	47"	Mahogany	24,450.
3809-S	47"	Polished Mahogany	25,550.
3819-S	47"	Walnut	20,995.
3819-S	47"	Polished Walnut	22,995.
3819-S	47"	Mahogany	20,995.
3819-S	47"	Polished Mahogany	22,995.
7708-S	47-1/2"	Polished Mahogany	10,750.
7708-S	47-1/2"	Polished Cherry	10,750.
7708-SCC	47-1/2"	*Custom Finish*	13,850.
7703-S	47-1/2"	Polished Mahogany	10,750.
7703-S	47-1/2"	Polished Cherry	10,750.
7703-SCC	47-1/2"	*Custom Finish*	13,850.
7707-U	48-1/2"	Ebony and Polished Ebony	11,595.
7707-U	48-1/2"	Walnut and Polished Walnut	12,550.
7707-U	48-1/2"	Polished Mahogany	12,550.
3817-U	50"	Polished Ebony	25,750.
3817-U	50"	Walnut	23,995.
3817-U	50"	Polished Walnut	26,850.
3817-U	50"	Mahogany	23,995.
3817-U	50"	Polished Mahogany	26,850.
7717-U	52"	Ebony and Polished Ebony	12,550.
7717-U	52"	Walnut and Polished Walnut	13,250.
7717-U	52"	Polished Mahogany	13,250.
Grands			
8501-B	5' 2"	Ebony and Polished Ebony	18,450.
8501-B	5' 2"	Walnut and Polished Walnut	19,350.
8501-B	5' 2"	Polished Mahogany	19,350.
8501-B	5' 2"	Polished Ivory/White	18,750.
8601-B	5' 2"	Ebony and Polished Ebony	25,995.
8601-B	5' 2"	Walnut and Polished Walnut	26,950.
8601-B	5' 2"	Polished Mahogany	26,950.
8601-B	5' 2"	Polished Ivory/White	26,250.
8601-M	5' 9-1/2"	"Classic" Ebony and Polished Ebony	20,595.

Model	Size	Style and Finish	Price*
8601-M	5' 9-1/2"	"Classic" Walnut and Polished Walnut	21,695.
8601-M	5' 9-1/2"	"Classic" Polished Mahogany	21,695.
8601-M	5' 9-1/2"	"Classic" Polished Ivory/White	21,150.
8701-M	5' 9-1/2"	"Classic" Ebony and Polished Ebony	27,495.
8701-M	5' 9-1/2"	"Classic" Walnut and Polished Walnut	28,395.
8701-M	5' 9-1/2"	"Classic" Polished Mahogany	28,395.
8701-M	5' 9-1/2"	"Classic" Polished Ivory/White	27,995.
8721-M	5' 9-1/2"	"Victorian" Ebony and Polished Ebony	22,995.
8721-M	5' 9-1/2"	"Victorian" Walnut and Pol. Walnut	23,750.
8721-M	5' 9-1/2"	"Victorian" Polished Mahogany	23,750.
8721-M	5' 9-1/2"	"Victorian" Polished Ivory/White	23,550.
8821-M	5' 9-1/2"	"Victorian" Ebony and Polished Ebony	29,750.
8821-M	5' 9-1/2"	"Victorian" Walnut and Pol. Walnut	30,695.
8821-M	5' 9-1/2"	"Victorian" Polished Mahogany	30,695.
8821-M	5' 9-1/2"	"Victorian" Polished Ivory/White	30,450.
8741-M	5' 9-1/2"	Polished Mahogany with Floral Inlays	28,995.
8741-MCC	5' 9-1/2"	*Custom Finish with Floral Inlays*	35,750.
8741-MCS	5' 9-1/2"	*Custom Finish with Custom Inlays*	on request
8731-M	5' 9-1/2"	Louis XV Ebony and Polished Ebony	25,995.
8731-M	5' 9-1/2"	Louis XV Walnut and Polished Walnut	26,895.
8731-M	5' 9-1/2"	Louis XV Polished Mahogany	26,895.
8731-M	5' 9-1/2"	Louis XV Polished Ivory/White	26,550.
4908-L	6'	"Euro Classic" Ebony	65,550.
4908-L	6'	"Euro Classic" Polished Ebony	68,095.
8701-L	6' 1"	"Classic" Ebony and Polished Ebony	22,250.
8701-L	6' 1"	"Classic" Walnut and Polished Walnut	23,095.
8701-L	6' 1"	"Classic" Polished Mahogany	23,095.
8701-L	6' 1"	"Classic" Polished Ivory/White	22,550.
8801-L	6' 1"	"Classic" Ebony and Polished Ebony	29,195.
8801-L	6' 1"	"Classic" Walnut and Polished Walnut	29,950.
8801-L	6' 1"	"Classic" Polished Mahogany	29,950.
8801-L	6' 1"	"Classic" Polished Ivory/White	29,250.
8709-L	6' 1"	"Victorian" Ebony and Polished Ebony	24,450.
8709-L	6' 1"	"Victorian" Walnut and Pol. Walnut	25,550.
8709-L	6' 1"	"Victorian" Polished Mahogany	25,550.
8709-L	6' 1"	"Victorian" Polished Ivory/White	24,750.
8809-L	6' 1"	"Victorian" Ebony and Polished Ebony	31,995.

*For explanation of terms and prices, please see pages 42–48.

Model	Size	Style and Finish	Price*

Schultz & Sons (continued)

8809-L	6' 1"	"Victorian" Walnut and Pol. Walnut	33,050.
8809-L	6' 1"	"Victorian" Polished Mahogany	33,050.
8809-L	6' 1"	"Victorian" Polished Ivory/White	32,950.
8811-X	6' 9"	Ebony and Polished Ebony	38,995.
8811-SX	7' 1"	Ebony and Polished Ebony	43,895.

Schulze Pollmann

Verticals

113	45"	Polished Ebony	8,390.
113	45"	Polished Peacock Ebony	9,190.
113	45"	Polished Briar Mahogany	9,190.
113	45"	Polished Peacock Mahogany	9,190.
113	45"	Polished Briar Walnut	9,190.
113	45"	Polished Peacock Walnut	9,190.
118/P8	46"	Polished Ebony	10,190.
118/P8	46"	Polished Briar Walnut	11,590.
118/P8	46"	Polished Feather Mahogany	11,590.
126/P6	50"	Polished Ebony	12,790.
126/P6	50"	Polished Peacock Ebony	13,790.
126/P6	50"	Polished Peacock Cherry	13,790.
126/P6	50"	Oval Feather Mahogany	13,790.
126/P6	50"	Polished Mahogany	13,790.
126/P6	50"	Polished Briar Mahogany	13,790.
126/P6	50"	Polished Peacock Mahogany	13,790.
126/P6	50"	Polished Sunburst Mahogany	13,790.
126/P6	50"	Polished Briar Walnut	13,790.
126/P6	50"	Satin and Polished Peacock Walnut	13,790.
126/P6	50"	Polished Sunburst Walnut	13,790.

Grands

160GK	5' 3"	Polished Ebony	25,990.
160GK	5' 3"	Polished Walnut	27,790.
160GK	5' 3"	Polished Briar Walnut	28,790.
160GK	5' 3"	Polished Mahogany	27,790.
160GK	5' 3"	Polished Briar Mahogany	28,790.

Model	Size	Style and Finish	Price*
160GK	5' 3"	Polished Ebony (round leg)	27,590.
160GK	5' 3"	Polished Walnut (round leg)	29,190.
160GK	5' 3"	Polished Mahogany (round leg)	29,190.
160GK	5' 3"	Chippendale Polished Walnut	32,590.
160GK	5' 3"	Chippendale Polished Mahogany	32,590.
160GK	5' 3"	With Renner Action, add'l	2,800.
190F	6' 2"	Polished Ebony	37,390.
190F	6' 2"	Polished Mahogany	39,990.
190F	6' 2"	Polished Briar Mahogany	42,390.
190F	6' 2"	Polished Walnut	39,990.
190F	6' 2"	Polished Briar Walnut	42,390.
197A	6' 7"	Polished Ebony	44,990.
197A	6' 7"	Polished Briar Mahogany	49,990.
197A	6' 7"	Polished Briar Walnut	49,990.

Seidl & Sohn

Prices do not include bench.

Verticals

Model	Size	Style and Finish	Price
SL 109	43"	Continental Polished Ebony	6,726.
SL 109	43"	Continental Polished Walnut	6,726.
SL 109	43"	Continental Polished Flame Mahogany	6,726.
SL 109	43"	Continental Polished White	6,873.
SL 113	46"	Polished Ebony	6,894.
SL 113	46"	Polished Walnut	6,894.
SL 113	46"	Polished Flame Mahogany	6,894.
SL 113	46"	Polished White	7,041.
SL 117	47"	Chippendale Polished Walnut	7,459.
SL 117	47"	Chippendale Polished Mahogany	7,459.
SL 120	48"	Polished Ebony	7,250.
SL 120	48"	Polished Walnut	7,250.
SL 120	48"	Polished Flame Mahogany	7,250.
SL 120	48"	Polished White	7,417.
SL 127	51"	Polished Ebony	8,276.
SL 127	51"	Polished Walnut	8,276.
SL 127	51"	Polished Mahogany	8,276.
SL 120/127		*Renner Action, add'l*	639.

*For explanation of terms and prices, please see pages 42–48.

Seiler

Verticals

Model	Size	Style and Finish	Price*
116	46"	"Mondial" Open-Pore Ebony	15,060.
116	46"	"Mondial" Open-Pore Walnut	15,060.
116	46"	"Mondial" Open-Pore Mahogany	15,060.
116	46"	"Mondial" Polished Mahogany	15,760.
116	46"	"Mondial" Open-Pore Oak	15,060.
116	46"	"Mondial" Open-Pore Maple	15,220.
116	46"	"Mondial" Open-Pore Cherry	16,040.
116	46"	"Mondial" Alderwood	15,220.
116	46"	"Mondial" Open-Pore Swiss Pear	15,540.
116	46"	"Mondial" Open-Pore Apple Heartwood	16,040.
116	46"	"Mondial" Polished Burl Rosewood	17,420.
116	46"	"Jubilee" Polished Ebony	16,160.
116	46"	"Jubilee" Polished White	16,420.
116	46"	Chippendale Open-Pore Walnut	15,220.
116	46"	"Escorial" Open-Pore Cherry, Intarsia	16,420.
122	48"	"Konsole" Open-Pore Ebony	15,680.
122	48"	"Konsole" Polished Ebony	16,740.
122	48"	"Konsole" Open-Pore Walnut	15,680.
122	48"	"Konsole" Polished Walnut Rootwood	22,660.
122	48"	"Konsole" Open-Pore Oak	15,680.
122	48"	"Konsole" Open-Pore Maple	15,680.
122	48"	"Konsole" Maple Burl	16,300.
122	48"	"Konsole" Open-Pore Cherry	16,440.
122	48"	"Konsole" Polished Burl Rosewood	19,360.
122	48"	"Konsole" Polished Brown Ash	19,360.
122	48"	"Konsole" Polished Redwood Burl	20,340.
122	48"	"Konsole" Polished White	17,300.
122	48"	"School" Open-Pore Ebony	14,960.
122	48"	"School" Open-Pore Walnut	14,960.
122	48"	"School" Open-Pore Oak	14,960.
122	48"	"Vienna" Polished Ebony w/Pilaster	17,200.
122	48"	"Vienna" Pol. Ebony w/Pilaster & Oval	17,360.
122	48"	"Vienna" Pol. Mahog. w/ Flower Inlays	19,360.
122	48"	"Vienna" Pol. Walnut w/ Flower Inlays	19,360.

Model	Size	Style and Finish	Price*
122	48"	"Vienna" Maple with Pilaster	17,200.
122	48"	"Vienna" Maple with Pilaster & Oval	17,360.
132	52"	"Concert SMR" Polished Ebony	21,320.
132	52"	"Concert SMR" Pol. Ebony w/Oval	21,960.
132	52"	"Concert SMR" Pol. Ebony w/Candle	21,920.
132	52"	"Concert SMR" Pol. Ebony w/Panels	22,060.
132	52"	"Concert SMR" Open-Pore Walnut	20,680.
132	52"	"Concert SMR" Polished Mahogany	21,980.
132	52"	"Concert SMR" Pol. Burl Rosewood	23,480.
132	52"	"Concert SMR" Polished Yew	25,280.
132	52"	"Concert SMR" Pol. Ash Rootwood	25,280.
132	52"	"Concert SMR" Polished Burl Maple	26,140.
132	52"	"Limited Edition" Polished Ebony	24,580.
132	52"	"Lim. Ed." Pol. Eby. w/Oval or Pilaster	25,080.
132	52"	"Lim. Ed." Pol. Eby. w/Oval & Pilaster	25,580.
Grands			
180	5' 11"	"Maestro" Polished Burl Rosewood	55,020.
180	5' 11"	"Maestro" Polished Flamed Maple	55,560.
180	5' 11"	"Maestro" Polished Peacock Maple	61,740.
180	5' 11"	"Maestro" Polished Canna Maple	61,740.
180	5' 11"	"Maestro" Polished Pyramid Mahogany	61,740.
180	5' 11"	"Westminster" Pol. Mahogany Intarsia	61,740.
180	5' 11"	"Florenz" Pol. Mahog./Myrtle Intarsia	61,740.
180	5' 11"	"Louvre" Polished Cherry Intarsia	61,740.
180	5' 11"	"Prado" Polished Brown Ash	63,480.
180	5' 11"	"Prado" Polished Burl Redwood	65,740.
180	5' 11"	"Stella" Pol. Maple Rootwood Intarsia	75,800.
180	5' 11"	"Concordia" Pol. Peacock Maple, Intarsia	75,800.
180	5' 11"	"Showmaster" Chrome/Brass/Polyester	122,960.
180	5' 11"	"Terrestre"	151,060.
180	5' 11"	"Suspension"	164,100.
186	6' 1"	"Maestro" Polished Ebony	47,180.
186	6' 1"	"Maestro" Open-Pore Walnut	47,180.
186	6' 1"	"Maestro" Polished Walnut	50,320.
186	6' 1"	"Maestro" Open-Pore Mahogany	47,180.
186	6' 1"	"Maestro" Polished Mahogany	50,320.
186	6' 1"	"Maestro" Polished Pyramid Mahogany	66,060.

*For explanation of terms and prices, please see pages 42–48.

Model	Size	Style and Finish	Price*

Seiler (continued)

Model	Size	Style and Finish	Price*
186	6' 1"	"Maestro" Polished Burl Rosewood	58,880.
186	6' 1"	"Maestro" Polished Flamed Maple	59,480.
186	6' 1"	"Maestro" Polished Peacock Maple	66,060.
186	6' 1"	"Maestro" Polished White	48,220.
186	6' 1"	Chippendale Open-Pore Walnut	50,200.
186	6' 1"	"Westminster" Pol. Mahogany, Intarsia	66,060.
186	6' 1"	"Florenz" Pol. Walnut/Myrtle, Intarsia	66,060.
186	6' 1"	"Florenz" Pol. Mahog./Myrtle, Intarsia	66,060.
186	6' 1"	"Louvre" Polished Ebony	52,960.
186	6' 1"	"Louvre" Polished Cherry, Intarsia	66,060.
186	6' 1"	"Louvre" Polished White	53,880.
186	6' 1"	"Prado" Polished Brown Ash	67,940.
186	6' 1"	"Prado" Polished Burl Redwood	70,360.
186	6' 1"	"Stella" Pol. Maple Rootwood, Intarsia	81,140.
186	6' 1"	"Meridian" Pol. Maple Rootwood Intarsia	81,140.
186	6' 1"	"Concordia" Pol. Maple Rootwood Intarsia	81,140.
186	6' 1"	"Showmaster" Chrome/Brass/Polyester	131,580.
208	6' 10"	Polished Ebony	54,220.
208	6' 10"	"Empire 1897" Open-Pore Blue w/Brass	167,700.
208	6' 10"	"Solitaire" Custom with Painting	189,020.
208	6' 10"	"Solitaire" Custom without Painting	153,460.
242	8'	Polished Ebony	73,700.

Sohmer (Persis International)

Verticals

Model	Size	Style and Finish	Price*
S-50	50"	Polished Ebony	9,300.
S-50	50"	Polished Mahogany	9,700.

Grands

Model	Size	Style and Finish	Price*
A	5' 3"	Polished Ebony	18,980.
A	5' 3"	Polished Mahogany	19,780.
B	5' 10"	Polished Ebony	21,980.
B	5' 10"	Polished Mahogany	22,780.
C	7' 2"	Polished Ebony	31,980.

Sohmer & Co. (SMC)

Verticals

Model	Size	Style and Finish	Price*
34F	42"	French Provincial Semi-Gloss Cherry	6,340.
34R	42"	Renaissance Semi-Gloss Walnut	6,340.
34R	42"	Renaissance Semi-Gloss Cherry	6,340.
34T	42"	Semi-Gloss Mahogany	6,340.
34T	42"	Semi-Gloss Walnut	6,340.

Grands

Model	Size	Style and Finish	Price*
50F	5'	French Prov. Semi-Gloss Mahogany	17,540.
50F	5'	French Provincial Semi-Gloss Cherry	17,540.
50T	5'	Ebony	14,340.
50T	5'	Semi-Gloss Mahogany	15,540.
50T	5'	Semi-Gloss Walnut	15,540.
50T	5'	Semi-Gloss Cherry	15,540.
63E	5' 4"	Empire Semi-Gloss Mahogany	19,740.
63E	5' 4"	Empire Semi-Gloss Walnut	19,740.
63E	5' 4"	Empire Semi-Gloss Cherry	19,740.
63F	5' 4"	French Prov. Semi-Gloss Mahogany	18,740.
63F	5' 4"	French Prov. Semi-Gloss Walnut	18,740.
63F	5' 4"	French Prov. Semi-Gloss Cherry	18,740.
63H	5' 4"	Hepplewhite Semi-Gloss Mahogany	17,740.
63H	5' 4"	Hepplewhite Semi-Gloss Walnut	17,740.
63H	5' 4"	Hepplewhite Semi-Gloss Cherry	17,740.
63T	5' 4"	Ebony	15,540.
63T	5' 4"	Semi-Gloss Mahogany	16,740.
63T	5' 4"	Semi-Gloss Walnut	16,740.
63T	5' 4"	Semi-Gloss Cherry	16,740.
77E	5' 9"	Empire Semi-Gloss Mahogany	20,340.
77E	5' 9"	Empire Semi-Gloss Walnut	20,340.
77E	5' 9"	Empire Semi-Gloss Cherry	20,340.
77F	5' 9"	French Prov. Semi-Gloss Mahogany	19,340.
77F	5' 9"	French Prov. Semi-Gloss Walnut	19,340.
77F	5' 9"	French Prov. Semi-Gloss Cherry	19,340.
77H	5' 9"	Hepplewhite Semi-Gloss Mahogany	18,340.
77H	5' 9"	Hepplewhite Semi-Gloss Walnut	18,340.
77H	5' 9"	Hepplewhite Semi-Gloss Cherry	18,340.

*For explanation of terms and prices, please see pages 42–48.

Model	Size	Style and Finish	Price*

Sohmer & Co. (continued)

Model	Size	Style and Finish	Price*
77T	5' 9"	Ebony	16,140.
77T	5' 9"	Semi-Gloss Mahogany	17,340.
77T	5' 9"	Semi-Gloss Walnut	17,340.
77T	5' 9"	Semi-Gloss Cherry	17,340.
90H	6' 2"	Hepplewhite Semi-Gloss Mahogany	18,540.
90H	6' 2"	Hepplewhite Semi-Gloss Walnut	18,540.
90H	6' 2"	Hepplewhite Semi-Gloss Cherry	18,540.
90T	6' 2"	Ebony	16,340.
90T	6' 2"	Semi-Gloss Mahogany	17,540.
95T	6' 8"	Ebony	22,350.
95T	6' 8"	Semi-Gloss Mahogany	23,350.
95T	6' 8"	Semi-Gloss Walnut	23,350.
95T	6' 8"	Semi-Gloss Cherry	23,350.

Steinberg, Gerh.

Verticals

Model	Size	Style and Finish	Price*
V-16HB	46"	Polished Ebony	5,090.
V-16HC	46"	Polished Mahogany	5,390.
V-16HC	46"	Polished Walnut	5,390.
V-16HC	46"	Polished Oak	5,390.
V-16HC	46"	Polished White	5,390.
V-16H/W	46"	Polished Ebony with Walnut Accents	5,090.
V-22BB	48"	Polished Ebony	5,990.
V-22BC	48"	Polished Mahogany	6,290.
V-22BC	48"	Polished Walnut	6,290.
V-22EB	48"	Queen Anne Polished Ebony	6,290.
V-22EC	48"	Queen Anne Polished Mahogany	6,590.
V-22EC	48"	Queen Anne Polished Walnut	6,590.

Grands

Model	Size	Style and Finish	Price*
S-159BB	5' 2"	Polished Ebony	15,890.
S-159BC	5' 2"	Polished Mahogany	16,490.
S-159BC	5' 2"	Polished Walnut	16,490.
S-159BC	5' 2"	Polished Ivory	16,490.
S-159BC	5' 2"	Polished White	16,490.

Model	Size	Style and Finish	Price*
S-186BB	6' 1"	Polished Ebony	17,990.
S-186BC	6' 1"	Polished Mahogany	18,890.
S-186BC	6' 1"	Polished Walnut	18,890.
S-186BC	6' 1"	Polished Ivory	18,890.
S-186BC	6' 1"	Polished White	18,890.

Steinberg, Wilh.

Prices depend on the exchange rate between the Euro and the U.S. Dollar. The prices below are based on Euro=$1.08.

Verticals

IQ 16	46"	Polished Ebony	9,340.
IQ 16	46"	Mahogany	11,234.
IQ 16	46"	Walnut	11,234.
IQ 16	46"	Oak	9,558.
IQ 16	46"	Cherry	10,156.
IQ 16	46"	Beech	9,558.
IQ 16	46"	Alder	9,558.
IQ 16	46"	Yew	10,156.
IQ 16	46"	"Amadeus" Polished Ebony	9,866.
IQ 22	49"	Polished Ebony	10,438.
IQ 22	49"	Mahogany	11,054.
IQ 22	49"	Walnut	11,054.
IQ 22	49"	Oak	10,652.
IQ 22	49"	Cherry	11,966.
IQ 22	49"	Beech	10,652.
IQ 22	49"	Alder	10,652.
IQ 22	49"	Yew	11,966.
IQ 22	49"	"Amadeus" Polished Ebony	12,670.
IQ 22	49"	"Amadeus" Mahogany	12,432.
IQ 22	49"	"Amadeus" Walnut	12,432.
IQ 28	52"	Polished Ebony	13,174.
IQ 28	52"	Mahogany	13,172.
IQ 28	52"	Walnut	13,172.
IQ 28	52"	Cherry	13,910.
IQ 28	52"	Yew	13,910.
IQ 28	52"	"Amadeus" Polished Ebony	14,474.

*For explanation of terms and prices, please see pages 42–48.

Model	Size	Style and Finish	Price*

Steinberg, Wilh. (continued)

Model	Size	Style and Finish	Price*
IQ 28	52"	"Amadeus" Cherry	15,480.
IQ 28	52"	"Passione" Polished Ebony	17,146.
IQ 28	52"	"Passione" Mahogany	17,148.
IQ 28	52"	"Passione" Walnut	17,148.
Grands			
IQ 77	5' 9"	Polished Ebony	32,604.
IQ 77	5' 9"	Mahogany	33,576.
IQ 77	5' 9"	Walnut	33,576.
IQ 77	5' 9"	Cherry	33,912.
IQ 99	6' 3"	Polished Ebony	40,696.
IQ 99	6' 3"	Mahogany	42,432.
IQ 99	6' 3"	Walnut	42,432.
IQ 99	6' 3"	Cherry	45,576.

Steingraeber & Söhne

This list includes only those models most likely to be offered to U.S. customers. Other models, styles, and finishes are available.

Verticals			
130	51"	Polished Ebony with "Twist" Panels	34,470.
138	54"	Polished Ebony	36,780.
138	54"	Polished Ebony with Wood Accents	40,810.
138	54"	Baroque	42,230.
Grands			
168N	5' 6"	Polished Ebony	55,200.
168K	5' 6"	"Classicism" Polished Ebony	65,420.
168K	5' 6"	"Classicism" Pol. Ebony w/Pyr. Mahogany	73,490.
168K	5' 6"	"Classicism" Pol. Ebony w/Burl Walnut	73,490.
205N	6' 9"	Polished Ebony	74,640.
205N	6' 9"	Polished Ebony with Pyr. Mahogany	78,670.
205N	6' 9"	Polished Ebony with Burl Walnut	78,670.
205K	6' 9"	"Classicism" Polished Ebony	84,340.

Steinlager

Verticals

Only prices for ebony (satin and polished) are shown here for verticals, but they are also available in ivory, white, natural, cherry, mahogany, brown, blue, oak, red, and walnut at additional cost.

Model	Size	Style and Finish	Price*
U09	42-1/2"	Ebony	2,781.
U09L	42-1/2"	Ebony	2,808.
U12T	44"	Ebony	2,942.
C12M	44"	Mediterranean Ebony	3,155.
C12M(D)	44"	Mediterranean Ebony	3,316.
C12F	44"	French Ebony	3,155.
C12F(D)	44"	French Ebony	3,316
C13M	44"	Mediterranean Ebony	3,369.
C13M(D)	44"	Mediterranean Ebony	3,530.
U19/U19T	46-3/4"	Ebony	2,995.
U19F	46-3/4"	French Ebony	3,075.
U20	46-3/4"	Ebony	3,262.
C19M	46-3/4"	Mediterranean Ebony	3,476.
C19M1	46-3/4"	"Special" Ebony	3,476.
C19M(D)	46-3/4"	Mediterranean Ebony	3,637.
C19M1(D)	46-3/4"	"Special" Mediterranean Ebony	3,637.
C19F	46-3/4"	French Ebony	3,476.
C19F(D)	46-3/4"	French Ebony	3,637
U22T	48-1/2"	Ebony	3,155.
U22T(D)	48-1/2"	Ebony	3,316.
U22F	48-1/2"	French Ebony	3,236.
U22F(D)	48-1/2"	Ebony	3,396.
U23T	48-1/2"	Ebony	3,316.
U23T(D)	48-1/2"	Ebony	3,476.
U23F	48-1/2"	French Ebony	3,396.
U23F(D)	48-1/2"	French Ebony	3,557.
U32T	52"	Ebony	3,316.
U32T(D)	52"	Ebony	3,476.
U32F	52"	French Ebony	3,396.
U32F(D)	52"	French Ebony	3,557.

*For explanation of terms and prices, please see pages 42–48.

Model	Size	Style and Finish	Price*

Steinlager (continued)

Grands

Model	Size	Style and Finish	Price*
XJ142	4' 8"	Polished Ebony	7,755.
XJ142	4' 8"	French Polished Ebony	7,755.
XJ142D	4' 8"	Polished Mahogany	7,915.
XJ142D	4' 8"	Polished Walnut	7,915.
XJ142D	4' 8"	Polished White	7,915.
XJ142F	4' 8"	French Polished Ebony	8,156.
XJ142FD	4' 8"	French Polished Mahogany	8,316.
XJ142FD	4' 8"	French Polished Walnut	8,316.
XJ142FD	4' 8"	French Polished White	8,316.
XJ152	5'	Polished Ebony	8,397.
XJ152D	5'	Polished Mahogany	8,557.
XJ152D	5'	Polished Walnut	8,557.
XJ152D	5'	Polished White	8,557.
XJ152F	5'	French Polished Ebony	8,798.
XJ152FD	5'	French Polished Mahogany	8,958.
XJ152FD	5'	French Polished Walnut	8,958.
XJ152FD	5'	French Polished White	8,958.
XJ162	5' 4"	Polished Ebony	9,252.
XJ162D	5' 4"	Polished Mahogany	9,413.
XJ162D	5' 4"	Polished Walnut	9,413.
XJ162D	5' 4"	Polished White	9,413.
XJ162F	5' 4"	French Polished Ebony	9,654.
XJ162FD	5' 4"	French Polished Mahogany	9,814.
XJ162FD	5' 4"	French Polished Walnut	9,814.
XJ162FD	5' 4"	French Polished White	9,814.
XJ172	5' 8"	Polished Ebony	9,894.
XJ172D	5' 8"	Polished Mahogany	10,055.
XJ172D	5' 8"	Polished Walnut	10,055.
XJ172D	5' 8"	Polished Oak	10,055.
XJ172D	5' 8"	Polished White	10,055.
XJ172F	5' 8"	French Polished Ebony	10,295.
XJ172FD	5' 8"	French Polished Mahogany	10,456.
XJ172FD	5' 8"	French Polished Walnut	10,456.
XJ172FD	5' 8"	French Polished White	10,456.

Model	Size	Style and Finish	Price*
XJ172FF	5' 8"	Rococo Polished Ebony	10,536.
XJ172L	5' 8"	Louis XV Polished Ebony	10,215.
XJ172LD	5' 8"	Louis XV Polished Ivory	10,376.
XJ187	6' 2"	Polished Ebony	10,616.
XJ187D	6' 2"	Polished Mahogany	10,777.
XJ187D	6' 2"	Polished Walnut	10,777.
XJ187D	6' 2"	Polished White	10,777.
XJ187F	6' 2"	French Polished Ebony	11,017.
XJ187FD	6' 2"	French Polished Mahogany	11,178.
XJ187FD	6' 2"	French Polished Walnut	11,178.
XJ187FD	6' 2"	French Polished White	11,178.
XJ187L	6' 2"	Louis XV Polished Ebony	10,937.
XJ187LD	6' 2"	Louis XV Polished Mahogany	11,098.
XJ187LD	6' 2"	Louis XV Polished Ivory	11,098.
XJ187FF	6' 2"	Rococo Polished Ebony	11,258.
XJ187FFD	6' 2"	Rococo Polished Mahogany	11,418.
XJ187FFD	6' 2"	Rococo Polished Walnut	11,418.
XJ187FFD	6' 2"	Rococo Polished White	11,418.

Steinway & Sons

Verticals

4510	45"	Sheraton Ebony	19,200.
4510	45"	Sheraton Mahogany	21,100.
4510	45"	Sheraton Walnut	21,800.
4510	45"	Sheraton Dark Cherry	22,500.
1098	46-1/2"	Ebony	18,200.
1098	46-1/2"	Mahogany	19,500.
1098	46-1/2"	Walnut	20,200.
K-52	52"	Ebony	23,800.
K-52	52"	Mahogany	26,800.
K-52	52"	Walnut	27,600.

Grands

S	5' 1"	Ebony	39,200.
S	5' 1"	Mahogany	43,700.
S	5' 1"	Walnut	45,000.
S	5' 1"	Figured Sapele	47,500.

*For explanation of terms and prices, please see pages 42–48.

Model	Size	Style and Finish	Price*

Steinway & Sons (continued)

Model	Size	Style and Finish	Price*
S	5' 1"	Dark Cherry	47,800.
S	5' 1"	Kewazinga Bubinga	48,800.
S	5' 1"	African Cherry	50,600.
S	5' 1"	Satinwood	53,600.
S	5' 1"	Santos Rosewood	54,400.
S	5' 1"	Pearwood	54,700.
S	5' 1"	East Indian Rosewood	55,400.
S	5' 1"	African Pommele	55,800.
S	5' 1"	Macassar Ebony	61,100.
S	5' 1"	Hepplewhite Dark Cherry	49,000.
M	5' 7"	Ebony	42,400.
M	5' 7"	Mahogany	47,500.
M	5' 7"	Walnut	48,800.
M	5' 7"	Figured Sapele	50,800.
M	5' 7"	Dark Cherry	51,200.
M	5' 7"	Kewazinga Bubinga	53,300.
M	5' 7"	African Cherry	54,000.
M	5' 7"	Satinwood	57,000.
M	5' 7"	Santos Rosewood	58,600.
M	5' 7"	Pearwood	59,000.
M	5' 7"	East Indian Rosewood	59,600.
M	5' 7"	African Pommele	60,000.
M	5' 7"	Macassar Ebony	65,600.
M	5' 7"	Hepplewhite Dark Cherry	53,500.
M 1014A	5' 7"	Chippendale Mahogany	58,000.
M 1014A	5' 7"	Chippendale Walnut	59,400.
M 501A	5' 7"	Louis XV Walnut	75,800.
M 501A	5' 7"	Louis XV East Indian Rosewood	88,000.
L	5' 10-1/2"	Ebony	47,300.
L	5' 10-1/2"	Mahogany	53,300.
L	5' 10-1/2"	Walnut	54,400.
L	5' 10-1/2"	Figured Sapele	56,700.
L	5' 10-1/2"	Dark Cherry	57,600.
L	5' 10-1/2"	Kewazinga Bubinga	59,600.
L	5' 10-1/2"	African Cherry	60,800.

Model	Size	Style and Finish	Price*
L	5' 10-1/2"	Satinwood	62,400.
L	5' 10-1/2"	Santos Rosewood	66,400.
L	5' 10-1/2"	Pearwood	66,800.
L	5' 10-1/2"	East Indian Rosewood	67,400.
L	5' 10-1/2"	African Pommele	67,700.
L	5' 10-1/2"	Macassar Ebony	73,700.
L	5' 10-1/2"	Hepplewhite Dark Cherry	60,000.
A	6' 2"	Limited Edition Tricentennial Pol. Eby.	75,700.
B	6' 10-1/2"	Ebony	60,000.
B	6' 10-1/2"	Mahogany	67,400.
B	6' 10-1/2"	Walnut	68,900.
B	6' 10-1/2"	Figured Sapele	72,000.
B	6' 10-1/2"	Dark Cherry	73,400.
B	6' 10-1/2"	Kewazinga Bubinga	75,400.
B	6' 10-1/2"	African Cherry	75,800.
B	6' 10-1/2"	Satinwood	76,200.
B	6' 10-1/2"	Santos Rosewood	83,800.
B	6' 10-1/2"	Pearwood	84,200.
B	6' 10-1/2"	East Indian Rosewood	85,000.
B	6' 10-1/2"	African Pommele	85,400.
B	6' 10-1/2"	Macassar Ebony	92,800.
B	6' 10-1/2"	Hepplewhite Dark Cherry	76,200.
D	8' 11-3/4"	Ebony	89,400.
D	8' 11-3/4"	Mahogany	97,900.
D	8' 11-3/4"	Walnut	99,500.
D	8' 11-3/4"	Figured Sapele	104,000.
D	8' 11-3/4"	Dark Cherry	105,900.
D	8' 11-3/4"	Kewazinga Bubinga	108,300.
D	8' 11-3/4"	African Cherry	110,900.
D	8' 11-3/4"	Satinwood	112,800.
D	8' 11-3/4"	Santos Rosewood	120,400.
D	8' 11-3/4"	Pearwood	120,800.
D	8' 11-3/4"	East Indian Rosewood	121,400.
D	8' 11-3/4"	African Pommele	121,700.
D	8' 11-3/4"	Macassar Ebony	132,900.
D	8' 11-3/4"	Hepplewhite Dark Cherry	110,200.

*For explanation of terms and prices, please see pages 42–48.

Steinway & Sons (continued)

Grands (Hamburg)

I frequently get requests for prices of pianos made in Steinway's branch factory in Hamburg, Germany. Officially, these pianos are not sold in North America, but it is possible to order one through an American Steinway dealer, or to go to Europe and purchase one there. The following list shows approximately how much it would cost to purchase a Hamburg Steinway in Europe and have it shipped to the United States. The list was derived by taking the published retail price in Europe, subtracting the value-added tax not applicable to foreign purchasers, converting to U.S. dollars (the rate used here is 1 Euro = $1.15 [$1.00 = .87 Euros], but is obviously subject to change), and adding approximate charges for duty, air freight, crating, insurance, brokerage fees, and delivery. Only prices for grands in polished ebony are shown here. *Caution:* This list is published for general informational purposes only. The price that Steinway would charge for a piano ordered through an American Steinway dealer may be different. (Also, the cost of a trip to Europe to purchase the piano is not included!)

Model	Size	Style and Finish	Price
S-155	5' 1"	Polished Ebony	48,800.
M-170	5' 7"	Polished Ebony	53,500.
O-180	5' 10-1/2"	Polished Ebony	57,100.
A-188	6' 2"	Polished Ebony	60,900.
B-211	6' 11"	Polished Ebony	70,500.
C-227	7' 5-1/2"	Polished Ebony	83,600.
D-274	8' 11-3/4"	Polished Ebony	114,600.

Story & Clark

Verticals

Model	Size	Style and Finish	Price
111	45"	Continental Polished Ebony	2,790.
111	45"	Continental Polished Red Mahogany	2,790.
112	45"	"Arlington" Oak	3,990.
112	45"	"Arlington" Fruitwood	3,990.
112	45"	"Arlington" Cherry	3,990.
113	45"	"Charleston" Oak	3,990.
113	45"	"Charleston" Fruitwood	3,990.
113	45"	"Charleston" Cherry	3,990.
114	45"	Polished Ebony	3,790.

Model	Size	Style and Finish	Price*
114	45"	Oak	3,790.
114	45"	Fruitwood	3,790.
115	45"	Queen Anne Polished Ebony	3,390.
115	45"	Queen Anne Polished Red Mahogany	3,390.
120	47"	Polished Ebony	3,990.
120	47"	Polished Red Mahogany	3,990.
120	47"	Polished Brown Mahogany	3,990.
140	53"	Polished Red Mahogany	5,990.
Grands			
152	5'	Polished Ebony	7,590.
152	5'	Polished Red Mahogany	8,190.
152	5'	Polished Brown Ribbon Mahogany	8,190.
152	5'	Polished White	8,190.
152S	5'	French Provincial Polished Ebony	8,790.
152S	5'	French Provincial Pol. Red Mahogany	9,390.
152S	5'	French Prov. Pol. Brn. Ribbon Mahogany	9,390.
152S	5'	French Provincial Polished White	9,390.
165	5' 5"	Polished Ebony	9,190.
165	5' 5"	Polished Red Mahogany	9,790.
165	5' 5"	Polished Brown Ribbon Mahogany	9,790.
185	6' 1"	Polished Ebony	11,590.
185	6' 1"	Polished Red Mahogany	12,190.
185	6' 1"	Polished Brown Ribbon Mahogany	12,190.

Strauss

Verticals

Model	Size	Style and Finish	Price*
UP-106	42"	Satin	3,590.
UP-108E	42-1/2"	Polished Ebony	3,190.
UP-108E	42-1/2"	Polished Mahogany	3,390.
UP-108E	42-1/2"	Polished Walnut	3,390.
UP-110A	43-1/2"	Polished Ebony	3,390.
UP-110A	43-1/2"	Polished Mahogany	3,590.
UP-110A	43-1/2"	Polished Walnut	3,590.
UP-110GD	43-1/2"	Satin	3,790.
UP-110GE	43-1/2"	Satin	3,790.
UP-117D,C	46"	Polished Ebony	3,590.

*For explanation of terms and prices, please see pages 42–48.

Model	Size	Style and Finish	Price*

Strauss (continued)

Model	Size	Style and Finish	Price*
UP-117D,C	46"	Polished Mahogany	3,790.
UP-117D,C	46"	Polished Walnut	3,790.
UP-118	46-1/2"	Polished Ebony	3,790.
UP-118	46-1/2"	Polished Mahogany	3,990.
UP-118	46-1/2"	Polished Walnut	3,990.
UP-120E	47"	Satin	4,990.
UP-120E2,3	47"	Polished Maple	5,190.
UP-120H	47"	Polished Ebony	4,990.
UP-122B	48"	Polished Ebony	3,990.
UP-122B	48"	Polished Mahogany	4,190.
UP-122B	48"	Polished Walnut	4,190.
UP-123	48"	Polished Ebony	5,390.
UP-125	49"	Polished Ebony	5,790.
Grands			
GP-170	5' 7"	Polished Ebony	11,990.

Suzuki

Model	Size	Style and Finish	Price*
Verticals			
AU-100	44-1/2"	Continental Polished Ebony	2,498.
AU-100	44-1/2"	Continental Polished Red Mahogany	2,498.
AU-200	46"	Polished Ebony	2,798.
AU-200	46"	Polished Red Mahogany	2,798.
AU-300	48-1/2"	Polished Ebony	2,998.
AU-300	48-1/2"	Polished Red Mahogany	2,998.
Grands			
AG-500	5'	Polished Ebony	7,980.
AG-500	5'	Polished Brown Mahogany	8,380.
AG-500	5'	Polished Red Mahogany	8,380.
AG-550	5' 5"	Polished Ebony	8,980.
AG-550	5' 5"	Polished Brown Mahogany	9,380.
AG-550	5' 5"	Polished Red Mahogany	9,380.

Vogel

Grands

Model	Size	Style and Finish	Price*
V-180M	5' 10"	Polished Ebony	21,980.
V-180M	5' 10"	Polished Mahogany	23,180.
V-180M	5' 10"	Polished Walnut	23,180.
V-180M	5' 10"	Polished White	23,180.
V-180C	5' 10"	"Classic" Polished Ebony	23,980.
V-180C	5' 10"	"Classic" Polished Mahogany	25,180.
V-180C	5' 10"	"Classic" Polished Walnut	25,180.
V-180C	5' 10"	"Classic" Polished White	25,180.
V-180C	5' 10"	Chippendale Polished Ebony	23,980.
V-180C	5' 10"	Chippendale Polished Mahogany	25,180.
V-180C	5' 10"	Chippendale Polished Walnut	25,180.
V-180C	5' 10"	Chippendale Polished White	25,180.

Walter, Charles R.

Verticals

Model	Size	Style and Finish	Price*
1520	43"	Oak	7,440.
1520	43"	Cherry	7,690.
1520	43"	Walnut	7,710.
1520	43"	Mahogany	7,850.
1520	43"	Riviera Oak	7,420.
1520	43"	Italian Provincial Oak	7,440.
1520	43"	Italian Provincial Walnut	7,730.
1520	43"	French Provincial Oak	7,730.
1520	43"	French Provincial Walnut	7,960.
1520	43"	French Provincial Cherry	7,980.
1520	43"	Country Classic Oak	7,480.
1520	43"	Country Classic Cherry	7,630.
1520	43"	Queen Anne Oak	7,790.
1520	43"	Queen Anne Cherry	7,980.
1520	43"	Queen Anne Mahogany	7,980.
1500	45"	Ebony	7,220.
1500	45"	Polished Ebony	7,590.
1500	45"	Oak	6,910.

*For explanation of terms and prices, please see pages 42–48.

Model	Size	Style and Finish	Price*

Walter, Charles R. (continued)

Model	Size	Style and Finish	Price*
1500	45"	Walnut	7,160.
1500	45"	Mahogany	7,360.
1500	45"	Cherry	7,340.
1500	45"	Gothic Oak	7,340.
Grands			
W-190	6' 4"	Ebony	31,980.
W-190	6' 4"	Semi-Polished and Polished Ebony	32,800.
W-190	6' 4"	Mahogany	33,400.
W-190	6' 4"	Semi-Polished and Polished Mahogany	34,240.
W-190	6' 4"	Walnut	33,400.
W-190	6' 4"	Open-Pore Walnut	32,600.
W-190	6' 4"	Semi-Polished and Polished Walnut	34,240.
W-190	6' 4"	Cherry	33,400.
W-190	6' 4"	Semi-Polished and Polished Cherry	34,240.
W-190	6' 4"	Oak	30,750.
W-190	6' 4"	Chippendale Mahogany	34,440.
W-190	6' 4"	Chip. Semi-Pol. and Pol. Mahogany	35,260.
W-190	6' 4"	Chippendale Cherry	34,440.
W-190	6' 4"	Chip. Semi-Pol. and Pol. Cherry	35,260.

Weber

Model numbers with two digits designate models from Korea, with three digits, from China.

Verticals

Model	Size	Style and Finish	Price*
W-109	43"	Continental Polished Ebony	3,100.
W-109	43"	Continental Polished Mahogany	3,190.
WF-108	43-1/2"	French Cherry	3,540.
WF-108	43-1/2"	Mahogany	3,540.
WF-108	43-1/2"	Italian Walnut	3,540.
WF-108	43-1/2"	Mediterranean Oak	3,540.
WFX-44	43-1/2"	French Cherry	5,990.
WS-46	46"	Ebony	4,990.
WS-46	46"	American Oak	5,190.
WS-46	46"	Walnut	5,190.

Model	Size	Style and Finish	Price*
W-121	48"	Polished Ebony	3,790.
W-121	48"	Polished Mahogany	3,990.
W-121	48"	Polished Walnut	3,990.
WF-121	48"	Walnut	4,190.
WSE-48	48"	Polished Ebony	6,390.
WSE-48	48"	Polished Mahogany	6,590.
WSE-48	48"	Polished Brown Mahogany	6,590.
W-131	52"	Polished Ebony	4,130.
W-131	52"	Polished Mahogany	4,330.
Grands			
WG-150	4' 11-1/2"	Polished Ebony	8,870.
WG-150	4' 11-1/2"	Polished Mahogany	9,070.
WG-150	4' 11-1/2"	Polished White	9,070.
WG-50	4' 11-1/2"	Queen Anne Cherry	15,990.
WG-157	5' 2"	Polished Ebony	9,990.
WG-157	5' 2"	Polished Mahogany	10,190.
WG-57	5' 7"	Ebony	15,790.
WSG-57	5' 7"	Queen Anne Polished Mahogany	18,990.
WSG-57	5' 7"	Queen Anne Cherry	18,990.
WG-175	5' 9"	Polished Ebony	11,390.
WG-175	5' 9"	Polished Mahogany	11,790.
WG-185	6' 1"	Polished Ebony	12,590.
WG-60	6' 1"	Ebony	17,390.
WSG-60	6' 1"	Polished Ebony	18,990.
WG-70	7'	Ebony and Polished Ebony	26,790.
WG-90	9'	Ebony and Polished Ebony	62,090.

Weinbach

Note: Prices below do not include bench. Add from $220 to $630 (most are under $400), depending on choice of bench.

Verticals

Model	Size	Style and Finish	Price
114-I	45"	Demi-Chippendale Polished Ebony	6,180.
114-I	45"	Demi-Chippendale Polished Walnut	6,180.
114-I	45"	Demi-Chippendale Pol.Flame Mahog.	6,180.
114-IC	45"	Chippendale Polished Ebony	6,500.
114-IC	45"	Chippendale Polished Walnut	6,500.

*For explanation of terms and prices, please see pages 42–48.

Model	Size	Style and Finish	Price*

Weinbach (continued)

Model	Size	Style and Finish	Price*
114-IC	45"	Chippendale Polished Flame Mahogany	6,500.
114-II	45"	Polished Ebony	5,500.
114-II	45"	Polished Flame Mahogany	5,500.
114-IV	45"	Polished Ebony	5,900.
114-IV	45"	Polished Walnut	5,900.
114-IV	45"	Polished Flame Mahogany	5,900.
124-III	50"	Polished Ebony	7,100.
124-III	50"	Polished Walnut	7,100.
124-III	50"	Polished Flame Mahogany	7,100.
Grands			
155	5' 3"	Polished Ebony	18,780.
155	5' 3"	Polished Walnut	18,780.
155	5' 3"	Polished Flame Mahogany	18,780.
170	5' 8"	Polished Ebony	19,800.
170	5' 8"	Polished Walnut	19,800.
170	5' 8"	Polished Flame Mahogany	19,800.
170 C	5' 8"	Chippendale Polished Walnut	23,800.
170 C	5' 8"	Chippendale Polished Mahogany	23,800.
192	6' 4"	Polished Ebony	23,000.
192	6' 4"	Polished Walnut	23,000.
192	6' 4"	Polished Flame Mahogany	23,000.

Wieler — see "Sängler & Söhne / Wieler"

Wurlitzer

Model	Size	Style and Finish	Price*
Grands			
WP 153	5' 1"	Ebony	11,580.
WP 153	5' 1"	Polished Ebony	10,990.
WP 153	5' 1"	Polished Mahogany	11,580.
WP 153	5' 1"	Walnut	10,990.
WP 153	5' 1"	Oak	10,990.
WP 153	5' 1"	Polished Ivory	10,990.
WP 153QA	5' 1"	Queen Anne Polished Mahogany	13,380.
WP 153QA	5' 1"	Queen Anne Oak	13,380.

Model	Size	Style and Finish	Price*
WP 153QA	5' 1"	Queen Anne Cherry	13,380.
WP 173	5' 8"	Ebony	12,990.
WP 173	5' 8"	Polished Ebony	12,390.
WP 173	5' 8"	Polished Mahogany	12,990.
WP 173	5' 8"	Polished White	12,390.

Wyman

Verticals

Model	Size	Style and Finish	Price*
WV96	37"	American Country Gallery Oak	2,790.
WV96	37"	French Provincial Sable Cherry	2,850.
WV99	39"	Continental Polished Ebony (73)	1,798.
WV99	39"	Continental Polished Cherry (73)	1,898.
WV108	42-1/2"	Continental Polished Ebony	2,550.
WV108	42-1/2"	Continental Polished Mahogany	2,590.
WV108	42-1/2"	Continental Polished Cherry	2,590.
WV110	43"	American Country Gallery Oak	2,970.
WV110	43"	Sable Brown Mahogany	2,970.
WV110	43"	French Provincial Sable Cherry	3,050.
WV110	43"	Country French Oak	3,050.
WV117	46"	Polished Ebony	2,900.
WV120	48"	Polished Ebony (straight legs)	3,150.
WV120	48"	Polished Mahogany (curved legs)	3,190.

Grands

Model	Size	Style and Finish	Price*
WG145	4' 9"	Polished Ebony	7,390.
WG145	4' 9"	Polished Mahogany	7,990.
WG150	4' 11"	Polished Ebony	7,790.
WG150	4' 11"	Polished Mahogany	8,190.
WG160	5' 3"	Polished Ebony	8,390.
WG160	5' 3"	Polished Mahogany	8,790.
WG170	5' 7"	Polished Ebony	8,990.
WG170	5' 7"	Polished Mahogany	9,390.

*For explanation of terms and prices, please see pages 42–48.

Model	Size	Style and Finish	Price*

Yamaha

Verticals

Model	Size	Style and Finish	Price*
M112	44"	Continental Ebony	5,090.
M112	44"	Continental Polished Ebony	5,190.
M112	44"	Continental American Walnut	5,290.
M112	44"	Continental Polished Mahogany	6,390.
M112	44"	Continental Polished Ivory/White	6,290.
M450	44"	American Oak	3,790.
M450	44"	Cherry	3,790.
M450	44"	Brown Cherry	3,790.
M475	44"	Mahogany	4,290.
M475	44"	Italian Provincial Cherry	4,290.
M500	44"	Chippendale Brown Mahogany	5,990.
M500	44"	Florentine Light Oak	4,890.
M500	44"	Georgian Mahogany	5,990.
M500	44"	Hancock Brown Cherry	4,290.
M500	44"	Milano Dark Oak	4,890.
M500	44"	Parisian Cherry	6,190.
M500	44"	Queen Anne Cherry	5,090.
M500	44"	Queen Anne Dark Cherry	5,090.
M500	44"	Sheraton Mahogany	4,290.
P22	45"	American Walnut	5,190.
P22	45"	Black Oak	5,190.
P22	45"	Dark Oak	5,190.
P22	45"	Light Oak	5,190.
T116	45"	Polished Ebony	5,390.
T116	45"	Polished Mahogany	6,390.
P600	45"	Sheraton Brown Mahogany	5,990.
P600	45"	Queen Anne Brown Cherry	5,990.
P600	45"	Tuscan Ash	6,190.
T121	48"	Polished Ebony	6,390.
U1	48"	Ebony	7,790.
U1	48"	Polished Ebony	7,990.
U1	48"	American Walnut	8,390.
U1	48"	Polished American Walnut	8,990.
U1	48"	Polished Mahogany	8,990.
U1	48"	Polished White	9,190.
U3	52"	Polished Ebony	10,690.
U3	52"	Polished Mahogany	11,990.

Model	Size	Style and Finish	Price*
U5	52"	Polished Ebony	12,590.
U5	52"	Bubinga	21,990.
Disklavier Verticals			
MX500	44"	Florentine Light Oak	9,790
MX500	44"	Georgian Mahogany	10,790.
MX500	44"	Milano Dark Oak	9,790
MX500	44"	Parisian Cherry	10,990.
MX500	44"	Parisian Dark Cherry	10,990
MX500	44"	Queen Anne Cherry	9,990.
MX500	44"	Queen Anne Dark Cherry	9,990.
MX22	45"	American Walnut	10,190.
MX22	45"	Dark Oak	10,190.
MX22	45"	Black Oak	10,190.
MX22	45"	Light Oak	10,190.
MX116	45"	Polished Ebony	10,390.
MX116	45"	Polished Mahogany	11,390
MX600	45"	Sheraton Brown Mahogany	10,990.
MX600	45"	Queen Anne Dark Cherry	10,990.
MX600	45"	Tuscan Ash	11,190.
MIDIPiano (Silent) Verticals			
MP500	44"	Florentine Light Oak	7,590.
MP500	44"	Georgian Mahogany	8,590.
MP500	44"	Hancock Brown Cherry	7,090.
MP500	44"	Milano Dark Oak	7,590.
MP500	44"	Parisian Cherry	8,790.
MP500	44"	Queen Anne Cherry	7,790.
MP500	44"	Queen Anne Dark Cherry	7,790.
MP500	44"	Sheraton Mahogany	7,090.
MP22	45"	American Walnut	7,790.
MPU1	48"	Polished Ebony	10,790.
Disklavier Verticals with Silent Feature			
DU1A	48"	Polished Ebony	15,790.
DU1A	48"	American Walnut	16,090.
DU1A	48"	Polished Mahogany	16,790.
DU1A	48"	Polished White	16,990.

*For explanation of terms and prices, please see pages 42–48.

Yamaha (continued)

Grands

Model	Size	Style and Finish	Price*
GA1E	4' 11"	Polished Ebony	9,990.
GC1	5' 3"	Ebony	14,490.
GC1	5' 3"	Polished Ebony	14,890.
GC1	5' 3"	American Walnut	16,490.
GC1	5' 3"	Polished American Walnut	16,490.
GC1	5' 3"	Polished Mahogany	16,490.
GC1	5' 3"	Polished Ivory	16,490.
GC1	5' 3"	Polished White	16,090.
GC1FP	5' 3"	French Provincial Brown Cherry	17,990.
GC1G	5' 3"	Georgian Brown Mahogany	17,990.
C1	5' 3"	Ebony	18,690.
C1	5' 3"	Polished Ebony	19,090.
C1	5' 3"	American Walnut	21,390.
C1	5' 3"	Mahogany and Polished Mahogany	22,190.
C1	5' 3"	Polished White	21,390.
C1	5' 3"	"Metro" Polished Ebony and Gold	23,390.
C2	5' 8"	Ebony	21,390.
C2	5' 8"	Polished Ebony	21,590.
C2	5' 8"	American Walnut	24,390.
C2	5' 8"	Polished American Walnut	25,190.
C2	5' 8"	Polished Mahogany	25,190.
C2	5' 8"	Light American Oak	24,390.
C2	5' 8"	Polished White	23,090.
C3	6' 1"	Ebony	29,090.
C3	6' 1"	Polished Ebony	29,290.
C3	6' 1"	American Walnut	32,090.
C3	6' 1"	Polished Mahogany	32,690.
C3	6' 1"	Polished White	31,990.
C3	6' 1"	NEO Aluminum and Cherry	83,990.
C3	6' 1"	Bubinga	55,990.
C3	6' 1"	Bubinga Floral	57,990.
C3C	6' 1"	*"Centennial" Pol. Mahog. w/Flower Inlays*	53,990.
S4	6' 3"	Polished Ebony	52,490.
C5	6' 7"	Ebony	31,390.
C5	6' 7"	Polished Ebony	31,590.
C5	6' 7"	Polished Mahogany	39,990.
C6	6' 11"	Ebony	34,790.

Model	Size	Style and Finish	Price*
C6	6' 11"	Polished Ebony	34,990.
C6	6' 11"	Polished Mahogany	41,990.
S6	6' 11"	Polished Ebony	59,390.
C7	7' 6"	Ebony	39,690.
C7	7' 6"	Polished Ebony	40,090.
C7	7' 6"	Polished Mahogany	46,090.
CFIIIS	9'	Polished Ebony	108,390.

Disklavier Grands

Model	Size	Style and Finish	Price*
DGA1E	4' 11"	Polished Ebony (playback only)	17,590.
DGC1	5' 3"	Polished Ebony (playback only)	23,390.
DGC1A	5' 3"	Ebony	28,130.
DGC1A	5' 3"	Polished Ebony	28,530.
DGC1A	5' 3"	American Walnut	30,130.
DGC1A	5' 3"	Polished American Walnut	30,130.
DGC1A	5' 3"	Polished Mahogany	30,130.
DGC1A	5' 3"	Polished Ivory	30,130.
DGC1A	5' 3"	Polished White	29,730.
DC1A	5' 3"	Ebony	32,330.
DC1A	5' 3"	Polished Ebony	32,730.
DC1A	5' 3"	American Walnut	35,030.
DC1A	5' 3"	Polished American Walnut	35,830.
DC1A	5' 3"	Mahogany and Polished Mahogany	35,830.
DC1A	5' 3"	Polished Ivory	34,390.
DC1A	5' 3"	Polished White	35,030.
DC1A	5' 3"	"Metro" Polished Ebony and Gold	37,030.
DC2A	5' 8"	Ebony	35,030.
DC2A	5' 8"	Polished Ebony	35,230.
DC2A	5' 8"	American Walnut	38,030.
DC2A	5' 8"	Polished American Walnut	38,830.
DC2A	5' 8"	Polished Mahogany	38,830.
DC2A	5' 8"	Polished Light American Oak	38,830.
DC2A	5' 8"	Polished White	36,730.
DC3A	6' 1"	Ebony	43,330.
DC3A	6' 1"	Polished Ebony	43,530.
DC3A	6' 1"	American Walnut	46,330.
DC3A	6' 1"	Mahogany and Polished Mahogany	46,930.
DC3CA	6' 1"	*"Centennial" Pol. Mahog. w/Flower Inlays*	63,990.
DC3A	6' 1"	NEO Aluminum and Cherry	98,230.
DC3A	6' 1"	Bubinga	70,230.
DC3A	6' 1"	Bubinga Floral	72,230.

*For explanation of terms and prices, please see pages 42–48.

Yamaha (continued)

DC5A	6' 7"	Ebony	45,630.
DC5A	6' 7"	Polished Ebony	45,830.
DC5A	6' 7"	Polished Mahogany	52,830.
DC6A	6' 11"	Ebony	49,030.
DC6A	6' 11"	Polished Ebony	49,230.
DC6A	6' 11"	Polished Mahogany	60,330.
DC7A	7' 6"	Ebony	53,930.
DC7A	7' 6"	Polished Ebony	54,330.

Disklavier Pro Grands

DC3APRO	6' 1"	Polished Ebony	51,490.
DS4APRO	6' 3"	Polished Ebony	76,890.
DC5APRO	6' 7"	Polished Ebony	53,790.
DC6APRO	6' 11"	Polished Ebony	57,190.
DS6APRO	6' 11"	Polished Ebony	83,790.
DC7APRO	7' 6"	Polished Ebony	64,090.
DCFIIISAPRO	9'	Polished Ebony	137,700.

MIDIPiano (Silent) Grands

MPC1	5' 3"	Polished Ebony	24,290.
MPC2	5' 8"	Polished Ebony	26,790.
MPC3	6' 1"	Polished Ebony	34,390.
MPC6	6' 11"	Polished Ebony	40,190.
MPC7	7' 6"	Polished Ebony	45,190.

Young Chang

See also under "Bergmann" and "Pramberger."

Verticals

GE-102	43"	Continental Polished Ebony	3,590.
GE-102	43"	Continental Polished Red Mahogany	3,700.
GE-102	43"	Continental Polished Brown Mahogany	3,700.
GE-102	43"	Continental Polished Ivory	3,590.
PE-102	43"	Continental Polished Ebony	3,560.
PE-102	43"	Continental Polished Red Mahogany	3,980.
PE-102	43"	Continental Polished Brown Mahogany	3,980.
GF-110	43-1/2"	Mahogany	4,440.
GF-110	43-1/2"	Queen Anne Oak	4,440.
GF-110	43-1/2"	Mediterranean Oak	4,440.